RACIST VIOLENCE
IN THE UNITED KINGDOM

Human Rights Watch/Helsinki

Human Rights Watch
New York · Washington · London · Brussels

ISBN 1-56432-202-5
Library of Congress Catalog Card Number: 96-77750

Addresses for Human Rights Watch
485 Fifth Avenue, New York, NY 10017-6104
Tel: (212) 972-8400, Fax: (212) 972-0905, E-mail: hrwnyc@hrw.org

1522 K Street, N.W., #910, Washington, DC 20005-1202
Tel: (202) 371-6592, Fax: (202) 371-0124, E-mail: hrwdc@hrw.org

33 Islington High Street, N1 9LH London, UK
Tel: (171) 713-1995, Fax: (171) 713-1800, E-mail: hrwatchuk@gn.apc.org

15 Rue Van Campenhout, 1000 Brussels, Belgium
Tel: (2) 732-2009, Fax: (2) 732-0471, E-mail: hrwatcheu@gn.apc.org

Web Site Address: http://www.hrw.org
Gopher Address://gopher.humanrights.org:5000/11/int/hrw
Listserv address: To subscribe to the list, send an e-mail message to majordomo@igc.apc.org with "subscribe hrw-news" in the body of the message (leave the subject line blank).

HUMAN RIGHTS WATCH

Human Rights Watch conducts regular, systematic investigations of human rights abuses in some seventy countries around the world. Our reputation for timely, reliable disclosures has made us an essential source of information for those concerned with human rights. We address the human rights practices of governments of all political stripes, of all geopolitical alignments, and of all ethnic and religious persuasions. Human Rights Watch defends freedom of thought and expression, due process and equal protection of the law, and a vigorous civil society; we document and denounce murders, disappearances, torture, arbitrary imprisonment, discrimination, and other abuses of internationally recognized human rights. Our goal is to hold governments accountable if they transgress the rights of their people.

Human Rights Watch began in 1978 with the founding of its Helsinki division. Today, it includes five divisions covering Africa, the Americas, Asia, the Middle East, as well as the signatories of the Helsinki accords. It also includes three collaborative projects on arms transfers, children's rights, and women's rights. It maintains offices in New York, Washington, Los Angeles, London, Brussels, Moscow, Dushanbe, Rio de Janeiro, and Hong Kong. Human Rights Watch is an independent, nongovernmental organization, supported by contributions from private individuals and foundations worldwide. It accepts no government funds, directly or indirectly.

The staff includes Kenneth Roth, executive director; Michele Alexander, development director; Cynthia Brown, program director; Barbara Guglielmo, finance and administration director; Robert Kimzey, publications director; Jeri Laber, special advisor; Lotte Leicht, Brussels office director; Susan Osnos, communications director; Jemera Rone, counsel; Wilder Tayler, general counsel; and Joanna Weschler, United Nations representative.

The regional directors of Human Rights Watch are Peter Takirambudde, Africa; José Miguel Vivanco, Americas; Sidney Jones, Asia; Holly Cartner, Helsinki; and Eric Goldstein, Middle East (acting). The project directors are Joost R. Hiltermann, Arms Project; Lois Whitman, Children's Rights Project; and Dorothy Q. Thomas, Women's Rights Project.

The members of the board of directors are Robert L. Bernstein, chair; Adrian W. DeWind, vice chair; Roland Algrant, Lisa Anderson, William Carmichael, Dorothy Cullman, Gina Despres, Irene Diamond, Fiona Druckenmiller, Edith Everett, Jonathan Fanton, James C. Goodale, Jack Greenberg, Vartan Gregorian, Alice H. Henkin, Stephen L. Kass, Marina Pinto Kaufman, Bruce Klatsky, Harold Hongju Koh, Alexander MacGregor, Josh Mailman, Samuel K. Murumba, Andrew Nathan, Jane Olson, Peter Osnos, Kathleen Peratis, Bruce Rabb, Sigrid Rausing, Anita Roddick, Orville Schell, Sid Sheinberg, Gary G. Sick, Malcolm Smith, Domna Stanton, Nahid Toubia, Maureen White, Rosalind C. Whitehead, and Maya Wiley.

CONTENTS

LIST OF TABLES

ACKNOWLEDGMENTS

This report was written by Carl Haacke, a consultant to Human Rights Watch/Helsinki. It was edited by Holly Cartner, executive director of Human Rights Watch/Helsinki, Dinah PoKempner, deputy counsel, and Jeri Laber, Special Adviser to Human Rights Watch.

Human Rights Watch/Helsinki wishes to thank Dev Berreh, Raju Bhatt, Deborah Coles, Unmesh Desai, Kapil Juj, Ranjit Lohia, Sajida Malik, Seilesh Mehta, Rahul Patel, Adil Rehman, Asad Rehman, Urmi Shah, and Helen Shaw.

This report was prepared for publication by Emily Shaw, associate with Human Rights Watch/Helsinki.

1. SUMMARY AND RECOMMENDATIONS

Racially motivated violence and harassment in the United Kingdom is a very serious problem and available figures show it is getting worse, not better. With 12,199 racially motivated incidents reported in fiscal year 1995/96, the United Kingdom has one of the highest levels of such incidents anywhere in Western Europe.

The level of racist incidents reported to the police has increased dramatically over recent years. Between 1989 and 1996 the number rose more than 275 percent, from 4,383 to 12,199. These already high figures, however, represent only a fraction of the actual level because many victims do not report crimes against them to the police. Estimates of the real figures based on the official British Crime Survey of 1991 indicate that approximately 32,500 violent assaults and an additional 26,000 acts of vandalism were racially motivated; overall, a full 18 percent of all crimes against ethnic minorities were considered to be racially motivated. This suggests that there is an ongoing crimewave perpetrated by some British whites against ethnic minority groups in the U.K. Ethnic minorities frequently report that they do not feel free because they are afraid of being viciously attacked by white racists.

There is a widespread impression among victims that the responsible authorities are failing effectively to investigate crimes against them. A disturbing number of individuals also recounted police brutality that appeared to have been racially motivated. Hostile or ineffective policing leaves many ethnic minorities frightened with no place to turn for protection. Eventually, many lose trust in the police and stop calling them for assistance, even when they are subjected to ongoing violence and harassment.

The degree to which ineffective policing is the result of racism, insufficient resources, poor policing at lower levels, or bad management at the upper levels is difficult to determine. Even in the best of circumstances, identifying, arresting, and convicting the perpetrator of every crime is a daunting task. As a result, victims can be left with the impression that their cases are not taken seriously, when in fact there are other barriers to successful prosecution. While it is important to recognize this reality, it does not adequately explain the numerous reports by ethnic minorities received by Human Rights Watch/Helsinki of lax investigations by police, nor does it justify hostile or brutal police practices frequently experienced by ethnic minorities.

The national government is outspoken against racially motivated violence and urges the police at all levels, as well as other state institutions, to respond effectively and decisively to such violence. Despite some positive policy initiatives by the government, there continue to be frequent reports of police who are

1

unwilling or unable to protect minority victims and cases of severe police brutality remain far too common. The extensive body of international and domestic law that prohibits racist violence and police misconduct is often violated in practice.

Recommendations

Human Rights Watch/Helsinki offers the following recommendations to protect ethnic minorities more effectively from racist violence and police brutality. The three categories of recommendations are aimed at: increasing the monitoring of incidents of racist violence and the response of various authorities at each stage; increasing accountability of those individuals and agencies that fail to respond effectively to racist violence; and establishing new initiatives or increasing the effectiveness of current initiatives in efforts to prevent and respond to racist violence.

Monitoring

- Although methods of monitoring racist violence at the divisional or subdivisional levels have improved greatly over recent years and the Crown Prosecution Service (CPS) has begun to evaluate some cases, Human Rights Watch/Helsinki recommends that a more systematized approach be established for both the police and CPS on a national scale in order to insure the most accurate findings.

Accountability

- To improve police practice and trust among ethnic minorities the police must be held accountable. As it stands, there is little evidence to indicate that the police are willing to crack down on individual officers who fail to uphold proper policing standards, and there is ample evidence to indicate that police brutality and misconduct often are not effectively investigated and/or go unpunished. British government officials have defended their response to racist violence by saying that their laws and policies are second to none. To be effective, however, these laws and policies must be enforced and methods of insuring accountability must be introduced.

- Current procedures for filing and investigating complaints of police misconduct are inadequate. The Police Complaints Authority (PCA) must become a truly independent investigative body to insure effective and trustworthy evaluation of police conduct. Police should not be investigating cases of police misconduct. In order to ensure thorough and unbiased investigations, Human Rights Watch/Helsinki urges that civilians be given substantial authority to investigate allegations of police misconduct either in conjunction with representatives of the PCA, or instead of it.

The current standard of proof — "beyond a reasonable doubt" — is an excessively high standard to apply uniformly to all acts of police misconduct. Human Rights Watch/Helsinki supports proposals to create a sliding scale system with higher standards for serious incidents and lower standards for lesser infractions.

Initiatives

- Police should improve relations and coordination with community groups and victim support groups.

- The Racial Incidents Units should improve staffing to ensure that cases are properly handled.

- A new law specifically targeting racist violence should be drafted and submitted to parliament.

- A more aggressive effort should be made to recruit black and other minority officers.

- Police officers should be provided with additional and improved training regarding racist violence.

- It must be carefully considered whether organized racial violence and harassment are categorically different from traditional crimes. In contrast to many other acts of violence and harassment, they are not random, but rather target particular ethnic groups in orchestrated campaigns to force vulnerable groups from their homes. In this context these crimes perhaps should be associated more with political terrorism than street crimes. While the new harassment laws do give the police improved tools to respond to individual acts of harassment, they do not recognize the possibility that the perpetrator has a prolonged history of racial violence and harassment.

2. A STATISTICAL OVERVIEW

Racially Motivated Violence

The level of racist violence reported to the police has increased steeply in recent years. Between 1989 and 1996, the number of incidents rose more than 250 percent from 4,383 to 12,199, with a dense concentration of racially motivated incidents in London. In Fiscal Year 1993/94, for example, 40 percent of all incidents reported in England and Wales took place in London. This can be explained by the fact that 45 percent of the minority population in England resides in the Greater London area, according to the 1991 census.[1]

RACIAL INCIDENTS REPORTED
TO THE POLICE IN ENGLAND AND WALES[2]

	1988	1989	1990	1991	1992	FY 93/94	FY 94/95	FY 95/96
Provinces	2.169	2.347	3.451	4.509	4.507	5.873	N/A	N/A
Met. (London)	2.214	2.697	2.908	3.373	3.227	5.124	N/A	N/A
England & Wales	4.383	5.044	6.359	7.882	7.734	10.997	11.878	12.199

Despite these unprecedented levels of reported crimes, the figures above are a significant underestimation of the actual level of racially motivated crimes because many victims do not report such crimes. According to one survey, 60 percent of victims did not report racially motivated incidents.[3] The government's

---

[1] Satnam Virdee. *Racial Violence and Harassment* (London: Policy Studies Institute, 1995), p 16.

[2] Ibid., p 15. A "racial incident" is defined in the study as: "Any incident in which it appears to the reporting or investigating officer that the complaint involves an element of racial motivation, or any incident that includes an allegation of racial motivation made by any person, whether the victim or a third party." This definition was adopted by the Association of Chief Police Constables and is generally used by all police divisions. Statistics for Fiscal Years 94/95 and 95/96 from a document submitted to Human Rights Watch/ Helsinki, November 20, 1996.

[3] Ibid., p. 16.

4

own British Crime Survey showed that in 1992, only 34 percent of blacks and 45 percent of Asians reported incidents that took place against them to the police.[4]

A detailed analysis of the 1991 British Crime Survey estimated that the actual figures were closer to 41,000 incidents against blacks and 89,000 against Asians, bringing the total number of incidents to 130,000. This shockingly high level of racially motivated incidents represents 5 percent of all criminal victimization and threats against all groups and 18 percent of the 730,000 crimes against ethnic minority groups. About 45 percent of these incidents were either violent assaults or vandalism, while 40 percent were threats.[5] All studies show that the majority of victims of racist violence are Asian.[6]

---

[4] Ibid. from N. Aye Maung and C. Mirrlees-Black, *Racially Motivated Crime: a British Crime Survey Analysis* (London: Home Office Research and Planning Unit, 1994), pp. 13-15. This is an increase in reporting over the 1988 figures, which showed that only 27 percent of Afro-Caribbeans and 39 percent of Asians reported incidents against them.

[5] Ibid., p. 25.

[6] The term "Asian" is commonly used in the U.K. to refer to minority populations originating primarily from Southern Asia, especially Bangladesh, India and Pakistan. Below is a breakdown of ethnic minority groups as a percentage of the regional population from the 1991 Census.

	Total Ethnic Minority	Black-Caribbean	Black-African	Indian	Pakistani	Bangladeshi	Chinese
Great Britain	4.26	0.90	0.38	1.53	0.87	0.30	0.29
England & Wales	4.59	0.99	0.41	1.66	0.91	0.32	0.29
England	4.81	1.04	0.43	1.75	0.96	0.34	0.30
Wales	0.93	0.11	0.09	0.23	0.20	0.13	0.17
Scotland	0.93	0.02	0.05	0.20	0.42	0.02	0.21
Greater London	15.36	4.30	2.42	5.20	1.31	1.28	0.85
Inner London	19.43	7.04	4.31	2.95	1.17	2.85	1.13

ESTIMATES OF ACTUAL LEVELS OF RACIALLY
MOTIVATED INCIDENTS BASED ON BRITISH CRIME SURVEY

Type of Incident	Percentage of total racist incidents	Number
Assault	25 percent	32,500
Vandalism	20 percent	26,000
Threats	40 percent	52,000
All crimes against minorities	18 percent	
—		
All criminal victimization and threats	5 percent[7]	

Patterns: Geography

There are significant regional differences in the degree to which racist incidents are reported. The variation may reflect actual differences in the levels of violence, differences in the willingness of victims to report, differences in the methods of monitoring violence, and/or differences in the density of the minority population being victimized. According to a report by the Preston Borough Council in 1992, 75 percent of ethnic minority households interviewed had experienced racist harassment in the past two years. By contrast, a 1993 survey by the London Research Center reported that 10 percent of ethnic minority households suffered racist harassment. Twenty-four percent of these incidents were physical assaults, 17 percent threats, and 64 percent verbal abuse.[8]

The following table is based on a Home Office document that was provided to Human Rights Watch/Helsinki on January 23, 1996:

---

[7] This figure indicates that 5 percent of all criminal victimization and threats involving any group are racially motivated; the vast majority being perpetuated by whites against Asians or Afro-Caribbeans.

[8] Home Affairs Committee, *3rd Report: Racial Attacks and Harassment, Vol. 1, 1994: Statements from Anti-Racist Alliance* (London: HMSO, 1995), p. 103.

REPORTED RACIST INCIDENTS BY POLICE FORCE AREA

Police force area	1989	1990	1991	1992	1993/94	1993/94[9]
Avon & Somerset	71	83	148	98	159	9
Bedfordshire	25	33	0	57	60	1
Cambridgeshire	60	71	107	110	100	6
Cheshire	0	0	3	29	98	17
Cleveland	55	57	68	73	50	6
Cumbria	4	1	9	7	14	12
Derbyshire	20	53	143	60	221	10
Devon & Cornwall	3	6	9	7	14	4
Dorset	12	3	9	10	25	9
Durham	23	41	70	40	32	12
Essex	26	43	59	80	133	7
Gloucestershire	20	51	25	33	28	4
Greater Manchester	40	123	204	401	658	5
Hampshire	50	42	141	139	212	11
Hertfordshire	49	51	0	106	117	4
Humbershire	52	67	81	68	79	14
Kent	81	88	120	56	160	6
Lancashire	93	201	116	231	262	5
Leicestershire	190	287	369	338	315	4
Lincolnshire	2	2	4	5	4	2
City of London	0	0	0	0	1	6
Merseyside	123	144	162	134	155	10
Metropolitan Police (London)	-	2,908	3,373	3,227	5,124	5
Norfolk	22	23	45	30	33	11
Northamptonshire	72	66	60	120	102	7
Northumbria	217	289	376	349	405	
North Yorkshire	6	12	20	22	22	8
Nottinghamshire	27	135	221	222	264	9
South Yorkshire	52	117	124	151	106	6
Staffordshire	44	101	158	95	117	8
Suffolk	62	74	75	55	73	12
Surrey	7	7	50	61	79	5
Sussex	141	92	98	98	214	22
Thames Valley	128	171	201	195	166	
Warwickshire	21	44	32	35	87	6
West Mercia	6	13	3	19	100	
West Midlands	169	268	445	379	487	1
West Yorkshire	306	254	322	218	244	2
Wiltshire	19	25	29	24	51	9
Dyfed Powys	0	0	0	0	0	
Gwent	4	5	12	31	21	5
North Wales	1	0	3	4	2	
South Wales	94	308	385	311	400	
Total	**2,397**	**6,359**	**7,882**	**7,734**	**10,997**	

---

[9] Number of incidents reported to police per 1,000 population ethnic minorities. Blanks occur when police areas do not coincide with census tracts.

REPORTS OF RACIAL INCIDENTS FOR EACH
POLICE FORCE AREA IN SCOTLAND FROM 1988 TO 1994/95[10]

Police Force	1988	1989	1990	1991	1992	1993	1994	FY 1994/95
Central	9	18	45	69	51	52	N/A	N/A
Dumfries & Galloway	0	0	0	0	0	4	N/A	N/A
Fife	0	0	3	35	30	20	N/A	N/A
Grampian	4	4	9	4	20	28	N/A	N/A
Lothian & Borders	89	91	178	213	184	223	N/A	N/A
Northern	N/A	N/A	N/A	N/A	N/A	1	N/A	N/A
Strathclyde	197	236	300	254	250	205	N/A	N/A
Tayside	N/A	27	101	103	128	193	N/A	N/A
Total	**299**	**379**	**636**	**678**	**663**	**726**	**791**	**832**

---

[10] Letter submitted by The Scottish Office-Crime Prevention Unit, July 14, 1995.

There are several community organizations that conduct monitoring of racist violence and assistance to victims. The following tables reflect some of their findings over the past few years.

GREENWICH ACTION COMMITTEE AGAINST RACIST ATTACKS (GACARA)[11]

Incident	1985	1986	1987	1988	1989	1990	1991	1992	1993	1994	1995
Murders	0	0	0	0	0	0	2	1	1	0	0
Police Harassment	7	11	8	12	18	20	54	61	33	26	26
Assaults	50	26	34	19	71	38	63	78	83	43	43
Damage to Property	182	169	153	147	190	149	209	268	269	294	273
Knives/Threats	29	20	14	16	18	15	21	32	21	22	25
Firearms	2	1	0	0	0	0	0	0	1	0	0
Airguns	2	2	0	1	6	3	4	0	1	9	0
Rubbish in letterbox[12]	35	37	54	41	42	41	59	262	178	129	129
Racist Abuse/ Threats	116	99	103	118	78	121	143	198	297	499	504
Total	**437**	**372**	**377**	**363**	**441**	**401**	**573**	**923**	**911**	**1018**	**1000**
Cases reported to police	85	55	68	102	136	162	304	367	376	400	383

---

[11] GACARA is a victim support group that covers the Greenwich borough in London with a population of 217,409, of which about 12.7 percent are ethnic minorities.

[12] It is very common for families to be abused on a regular basis in their homes by their white neighbors who wish to drive them out of the community. One method of harassment is to stuff things such as feces and urine through the letter box.

NEWHAM MONITORING PROJECT (NMP)

Incident	1989	1990	1992/93	1993/94	1994/95
Murder	0	0	1	1	1
Physical assault/abuse	51	74	78	64	72
Verbal abuse/threats	56	49	72	79	87
Arson/Damage to Property	0	5	9	66	58
Assault by Police	39	28	35	34	34
Verbal abuse by Police[13]	24	25	26	30	30
Other	31	35	38	21	35
TOTAL	**201**	**216**	**259**	**295**	**317**

Although the police figures show a steady and rapid increase in racially motivated incidents, some analysts have argued that this change reflects a greater level of reporting due to police and community initiatives, not necessarily an increase in the actual level of racist violence.

While it is true that there has been an increase in the reporting of racially motivated violence, due in part to government efforts to document such crimes more effectively, it is doubtful that this accounts for the entire increase.[14] Local community groups and individuals uniformly reported to Human Rights Watch/Helsinki that racist violence was rising dramatically.

---

[13] According to NMP, reports of racially motivated police abuse often implicate some police stations more than others. For example, in 1994, NMP received fifty-nine complaints against Forest Gate, fifty-one against Plaistow, forty-six outside the borough of Newham, five against East Ham and thirty-five were unclear. These figures represent complaints made to NMP, not substantiated charges of police misconduct. Some cases indicated hostile interaction with the police, but not all reflected clear human rights abuses. NMP received thirty-four complaints of assault at the hands of police in a single borough within one year.

[14] The Policy Studies Institute (PSI) showed that from 1988 to 1992 the percentage of Afro-Caribbeans reporting racially motivated crimes rose 7 percent from twenty-seven to thirty-four and the percentage of Asians reporting such crimes rose 6 percent from thirty-nine to forty-five. Thus the increased reporting contributed to an estimated 13 percent growth in racially motivated crime. The police figures, however, show that racist incidents increased 200 percent over the same period. This suggests that the remaining increase was due to factors other than increased reporting. At least some of the increase not accounted for by higher reporting appears to reflect an increase in the level of violence.

Patterns: Perpetrators/Victims

Racially motivated violence and harassment are often part of a general campaign intended to force Asian and Afro-Caribbean families to leave their homes. A Home Office study of east London found that 66 percent of minority ethnic families suffered repeat victimization.[15] In the study, twenty-three Bengali and Somali families reported suffering 136 incidents within a six-month period. Most families were harassed an average of every nine days. Six of these families suffered twelve to twenty-seven incidents within a six-month period.[16] Similarly, another study documented 724 incidents against 114 families interviewed or about six incidents per family during the same six-month period.[17]

The Newham Monitoring Project reported that 149 of their cases in 1994/95 took place at the victim's home. This compares to seventeen at work, twelve at school and seventy-five on the street.[18]

Victims also frequently report that they know the perpetrators. In a study that covered the Newham area of London, 77 percent knew the individuals involved.[19]

---

[15]A. Sampson and C. Phillips, *Multiple Victimization: racial attacks on an east London estate* (London: Home Office Police Department, 1992), p. 5-6.

[16] Ibid., p. 22.

[17] Home Affairs Committee, 3rd Report: Racial Attacks and Harassment, Vol. 1, 1994, p.141.

[18] Newham Monitoring Project, *Annual report for Newham Monitoring Project 1994/95* (London:1995), p.6.

[19] Jeremy Cooper and Tarek Qureshi, *Through Patterns Not Our Own* (London: University of East London, New Ethnicities and Education Group, 1993), p. 51.

PATTERNS: VICTIMS
Percent of incidents seen as racially motivated:
1988, 1992 British Crime Surveys[20]

	Afro-Caribbean		Asian	
	1988	1992	1988	1992
Assault	34	24	36	56
Threats	44	24	50	66
Vandalism	20	23	32	26
All	15	13	24	24

PATTERNS: PERPETRATORS

Racial Incidents Carried Out by:	Percentage of Total Racial Incidents [21]
Males	73.7
Females	3.3
Both	13.9
People aged 15-25	68
Acted as a group	69
Acted alone	20.6
White	90
Afro-Caribbean	0.5
Mixed race group	2.9

---

[20] Virdee, *Racial Violence*, p 18; Aye Maung and Mirrlees-Black *Racially Motivated Crime*, p 13.

[21] Home Affairs Committee, *3rd Report: Racial Attacks and Harassment*, p.140.

Less research has been conducted on the level of racist violence in Northern Ireland. One study among 7,000 Chinese reported that 90 percent suffered physical violence or verbal abuse.[22]

There are reports of anti-Irish incidents in England, although this phenomenon has not been researched thoroughly. One study, *Crime Policing and the Irish Community in Southward South London,* indicated that 44 percent of those surveyed had suffered harassment because of their ethnicity. Twenty-six percent of these suffered physical attacks, and 7 percent had their homes attacked.

Additionally, there are some reports of incidents of anti-Semitism. In 1992 there were 281 recorded crimes motivated by anti-Semitism, 239 of which were in London. This represents a decrease from 387 in 1991. Jewish groups interviewed did not highlight violence as a major concern for their community, but were concerned about increasing anti-Semitic rhetoric.[23]

Radical Right Groups

The British National Party (BNP) is an openly racist and nationalist party with a history connecting it to active neo-Nazi organizations. In September 1993, the BNP unexpectedly won its first political campaign in a by-election for a city council seat in the Millwall area of East London, after years of rarely polling more than 5 percent. Although the BNP lost this seat in May 1994, it has since frequently polled between 10-20 percent. While the British National Party is not considered directly responsible for a large degree of racist violence, it does recruit from skinhead and football hooligan groups that are involved in racist violence, and many believe that the party encourages racist violence.[24] Additionally, several leading members and supporters of the British National Party have criminal records for racially motivated crimes.

There is evidence that the BNP efforts to mobilize voters and activists does increase violence in ethnic communities. During the month of January 1994, following the first election victory of a BNP candidate, the number of reported

---

[22]Ciaran Byrne and Tim Rayment, "Asian chained and abused in 'racist' Ulster," *Sunday Times (London)*, April 23, 1995.

[23] Human Rights Watch/Helsinki interview with Michael Whine, Board of Jewish British Deputies, London, June 15, 1996.

[24] Human Rights Watch/Helsinki interviews with Tony Robson, *Searchlight*, London, June and July 1995.

racist incidents increased by 300 percent in that area compared to January 1993.[25] Between 1991 and 1992, when the BNP established its headquarters in the Plumstead area of South East London, there was a 61 percent increase in the number of reported cases of racist violence[26] as well as four racially motivated murders.[27] The increase in this area took place at a time when violence in London was generally decreasing and there had been no reports of racist murders for many years.

While members of the BNP have been involved in a number of incidents of racist violence, the BNP attempts to present itself as a political party that seeks to gain support through democratic elections. Estimates of official BNP membership range from 1,500 to 2,500.

The leader of the BNP, John Tyndall, was convicted for a series of offenses in the 1960s ranging from assault to organizing and participating in paramilitary neo-Nazi activities. In 1986, he was convicted and sentenced to twelve months of imprisonment for conspiracy to publish material likely to incite racist hatred.[28]

The national campaign organizer, Richard Edmunds and two other important members of the BNP were convicted of malicious wounding in September 1993 for their involvement in the stabbing of a black man. In an earlier incident in 1992, Edmunds was convicted of "affray"— bodily harm.[29]

---

[25] There were seventeen reported attacks on the Isle of Dogs in January 1993 compared to fifty-seven for January 1994."Racist Wave Sweeps East End," *The Observer*, February 13, 1994.

[26] Greenwich Action Committee Against Racist Attacks reported that between 1991 and 1992 there was a 61 percent increase in racially motivated incidents.

[27] Roland Adams, fifteen years old, February 1991; Orville Blair, twenty-five years old, May 1991; Rohit Duggal, sixteen years old, July 1992; Stephen Lawrence, April 1993. *Home Affairs Committee, 3rd Report: Racial Attacks*, p. 197. Following the murder of Roland Adams, the BNP publicly congratulated whites for "defending their estate" in leaflets distributed through the new town. See also "Murders in 1991" section of the chapter on Racial Murders.

[28] Human Rights Watch/Helsinki interview with Tony Robson of *Searchlight*, London, July 10, 1995.

[29]Ibid.

Another leading organizer, Anthony Lecomber, was convicted under the Explosives Act for exploding a nail bomb and possessing hand grenades[30] in 1987 and was sentenced to three years of imprisonment. In 1990, he was convicted for bodily harm and in 1991 he was sentenced again to three years for assaulting a Jewish teacher.

It is the explicit aim of the militant group, Combat 18 (C18), to incite a race war. It has produced newsletters listing the names and addresses of individuals to be targeted for attack or murder. These lists include leftist, anti-racist and anti-fascist activists, as well as members of the Jewish, Asian and Afro-Caribbean communities. Accompanying these lists are instructions for making bombs and other weapons.

The language is explicitly *intended* to incite racist violence and terrorism. The periodicals have also been found in the hands of people who have carried out attacks on individuals listed, indicating that the language is also *able* to incite racist violence.

For example, above a list of names and addresses, there are phrases such as, "Death to Race Traitors," "Wanted Dead For Treason," "Exterminate 'Em," "Kill 'Em," and "Kill 'Em All." In numerous cases, articles will praise reported incidents of racist violence or murder, claim responsibility, and/or encourage others to do the same.

One periodical with the heading "The White Wolves," which is thought to have been produced by Combat 18, describes in detail why racist violence is important to their political goals and encourages participation.

Simon Chadwick along with three other British National Party (BNP) members attacked a prominent Jewish solicitor, **Danny Phillips**, in Mansfield, Nottinghamshire. Before this incident Mr. Phillips and his family had been regularly harassed. Numerous phone callers had threatened to burn his family out of their home. BNP stickers had been placed over his office and a rock had been thrown through the window of his home. While investigating the assault on him, police found a C18 periodical on one of his assailants that listed Mr. Phillip's address and phone number with the caption, "Dead enemies are the best propaganda: the future belongs to us." The newsletter also published a list of Jewish students with their names and phone numbers and described them as "hooked-nosed vermin."[31]

---

[30] Martyn Harris, *Daily Telegraph*, September 29, 1993.

[31] Sally Weale, "Neo-Nazis Focus on New Combat Zone," *The Guardian*, February 12, 1994.

Numerous other incidents show that militant groups frequently carry out violent acts against ethnic minorities and political activists who oppose racism and racist politics. Below are some examples:

- In 1995, in the city of Kent, a fire was set in the house of **Jill Emerson**. She had been an active anti-fascist campaigner in the area. After one campaign, her name appeared in a periodical similar to that of Combat 18's called "Target." Police are treating the case as attempted murder.[32]

- On December 1, 1994, **Gerry Gable**, the editor of *Searchlight*, and a leading investigator into fascist organizations was sent a letter bomb, which was discovered and did not explode.

- On January 15, 1994, a gang of skinheads attacked **Mushroom Books**, a left-wing bookshop in Nottingham. In the planned attack, they stormed the shop attacking the staff, visitors and causing thousands of pounds of damage. The store manager was knocked unconscious. The police were reportedly quick to respond, arresting eleven of the gang who were only charged and convicted with threatening behavior and a sentence of two months. The court heard that those individuals who caused the most significant damage were not apprehended.[33]

In another case, members of C18 and the National Socialist Alliance severely beat two women. Although there were two witnesses from Grenada television, it took three weeks to interview one of them, while the second was never questioned.[34]

According to Michael Whine of the Institute of Jewish Affairs and Tony Robson of the Searchlight Information Service, which reports on fascist activity, investigations and prosecutions of Combat 18 activity have been very slow.

The homes of several leading C18 members were raided in January and March 1995. But according to Mr. Whine and Mr. Robson, the clues found during these raids were not being acted upon promptly by the CPS or the attorney general. The individuals targeted in the raids were not held in custody, but were charged with possession of racially inflammatory material. They also said that findings

---

[32] *Searchlight*, May 1995.

[33] *Searchlight*, March 1995.

[34] *Searchlight*, May 1995.

from a raid on one of the figures a year ago is still languishing in the offices of the CPS.

William James Browning, twenty-five years old, and Paul David Sargent, thirty-five years old, are currently facing six charges of conspiracy and possession of material likely to incite racial hatred. Tony Robson of *Searchlight* considered these charges excessively light because these figures have a long established relationship with the militant C18. Under the current charges they face a maximum sentence of two years for each charge.[35] They face trial, along with Martin Cross in March 1997. In January, 1997, Mark Atkinson and Robin Grey were charged with publishing "hit lists" in *The Stormer*.[36]

CONVICTIONS OF MEMBERS OF
FAR-RIGHT ORGANIZATIONS FOR HATE CRIMES[37]

As of June 1995

#	Group	Charge	Place	Sentence
13	C18	Threatening behavior/ violent disorder	Nottingham	38 months
1	C18	Actual bodily harm	London	30 months
6	C18	Causing damage to Irish pub	London	1 year
4	C18	Attacked Chinese restaurant staff	Gr. Manchester	9-16 mon.
1	-	Wounding with intent	London	8 years
1	-	Racial abuse/attacking with dog	London	1 year
3	BNP	Attacked Labor Party member[38] and mixed race youth	Teeside	2 years

---

[35] If convicted of all charges, the sentencing judge could opt to run these maximum sentences consecutively for a total of twelve years.

[36] Document submitted by Michael Whine of the Board of Deputies of British Jews, February 19, 1997.

[37] The list is not exhaustive. BNP = British National Party; C18= Combat 18; NF = National Front; BNSM = British National Socialist Movement. Members of the British National Party and Combat 18 (C18) have also been convicted for many other offenses that are not racially motivated. These range from attacks on left-wing activists, drug charges, weapons charges, to disorderly conduct. C18 has approximately 120 core members. The right-wing militant group was once a wing of the BNP but has since split over internal disputes. Participating in and stirring up racist violence is an articulated strategy of Combat 18. Although there is no way to measure the impact of this plan, the group's members have been convicted and associated with several attacks on ethnic minorities and left-wing activists.

[38] During campaign for the BNP.

1994

5	BNP	Attacked Omani Airmen	Blackpool	1 year/100 hrs svc.
1	-	Murder of Sudanese refugee	Brighton	Life
4	C18	Threatened woman in her home	Chelsea	2 years keeping the peace[39]
1	C18	Threatening words and behavior	Leeds	3 months
2	-	Grievous bodily harm	Birmingham	13 years
2	BNP	Burglary/arson	Blackpool	2 years
1	BNP	Actual bodily harm	Northampts.	1 year keeping the peace
1	-	wounding with intent to cause GBH	Hartlepool	7 years
1	BNSM	Possession of firearms/conspiracy to carry out armed robbery	Hucknall	78 months
3	-	Stabbed & ran over black man	London	5-7 years
3	NF/ BNP	Assault, abductions & possessing illegal firearms	Blackpool	1-3 years
1	-	Violent rampage	Richmond	4 years
1	NF	Possession of firearms	Scotland	54 months
3	BNP	Violent disorder	London	51 months[40]
1	C18	Violence	London	9 months
3	BNP	Violent disorder	Sunderland	18 months,3 years
1	BNP	Assault	Newcastle	12 months

1993

3	BNP	Criminal damage	London	-
1	-	Murder	Manchester	2 life sentences
1	-	Murder	Manchester	Life (At Her Majesty's Pleasure)
2	-	Manslaughter	Manchester	12-13 years
3	-	Murder of Rahullah Aramesh	London	Life
1	BNP	Affray	Mansfield	120 hours[41]

---

[39] "Avoiding a breach of the peace, dissuading or preventing others from breaking the peace." Henry Black, *Black's Law Dictionary*, (St. Paul: West Publishing, 1983) p. 449.

[40] Committed by leading figures in the BNP. Richard Edmunds, national organizer, received a three-month sentence; Steven O'Shea received twelve months; Simon Biggs received four years, six months.

[41] Simon Chadwick.

RECENT ELECTION RESULTS IN
KEY AREAS INDICATING RADICAL RIGHT SUPPORT[42]

Date	Authority	Ward	Party	% vote
02.05.96	Stoke on Trent	Brownhills	BNP	5.40
02.05.96	Sandwell	Tipton Green	Nat/Dem	8.31
02.05.96	Dudley	Castle & Priory	Nat/Dem	12.20
02.05.96	Cannock	Norton Canes	Nat/Dem	5.96
02.05.96	Cannock	Heath Hayes	Nat/Dem	6.98
21.11.95	Newham	Forest Gate	BNP	5.32
09.11.95	Tower Hamlets*		BNP	6.41
19.10.95	Ashfield County*		BNP	5.65
21.09.95	Cannock Chase*		Nat/Dem	10.55
23.02.95	Tower Hamlets*		BNP	16.90
26.1.95	Newham*	South Beckton	BNP	12.87
15.12.94	Tower Hamlets*	Landsbury	BNP	19.47
15.9.95	Tower Hamlets*	Shadwell	BNP	12.30
5.5.94	Tower Hamlets	Millwall	BNP	9.00
5.5.94	Tower Hamlets	Millwall	BNP	10.35
5.5.94	Tower Hamlets	Millwall	BNP	8.69
5.5.94	Tower Hamlets	St. James	BNP	12.33
5.5.94	Tower Hamlets	Holy Trinity	BNP	7.91
5.5.94	Tower Hamlets	Holy Trinity	BNP	7.48
5.5.94	Tower Hamlets	Holy Trinity	BNP	7.42
5.5.94	Tower Hamlets	St. Peters	BNP	8.07
5.5.94	Hertfordshire	Rosedale	BNP	10.07
5.5.94	Hertfortshire	Redbourne	IND	18.81
5.5.94	Lewisham	Hither Green	CON (ex-NF)[43]	10.16
5.5.94	Newham	Beckton	BNP	16.49
5.5.94	Newham	Beckton	BNP	16.42
5.5.94	Newham	Custom House	BNP	8.45
5.5.94	Newham	Custom House	BNP	7.48
5.5.94	Newham	Custom House	BNP	8.20
5.5.94	Dudley	Lye & Wollescote	NF	10.31
16.9.94	Tower Hamlets*	Millwall	BNP	33.86
1.10.92	Tower Hamlets	Millwall	BNP	20.00

---

[42]Document submitted by Michael Whine of the Board of Deputies of British Jews, February 19, 1997. Only those elections in which the party reached 5 percent of the vote are listed.

[43] Barry James Olley ran as a member of the Conservative Party but has been connected with the British Movement and National Front.

While the overall number of far-right candidates has dropped by half, the percentage of the total vote received by far-right candidates has increased more than 600 percent.

OVERALL SUPPORT FOR NF AND BNP[44]

	BNP		NF		Both	
Year	# of candidates	% of total vote	# of candidates	% of total vote	# of candidates	% of total vote
1982	1	0.31	65	2.57	66	2.88
1986	6	1.96	27	3.28	33	5.24
1990	11	2.29	2	1.88	13	4.17
1994	29	13.17	15	5.04	34	18.21

---

[44]Document submitted by Michael Whine of the Board of Deputies of British Jews, July 14, 1995.

3. RACIALLY MOTIVATED MURDERS

Racially motivated violence has led to brutal murders in a number of cases. Although such murders remain relatively rare, each murder produces a new wave of anxiety and fear for communities that already feel perpetually threatened. Human Rights Watch/ Helsinki heard numerous accounts of ethnic minorities who live in daily fear that the violence and harassment they frequently experience could at any moment lead to death.

Murders in 1994

Mohan Singh Kullar, sixty years old, was the victim of racially motivated harassment and attacks over a period of weeks in his shop in Neath, South Wales. On November 27, 1994, Mr. Kullar was killed by a gang of three white youths. They lured him outside his store, smashed his head with a brick, and beat him until he was unconscious. He died in the hospital on December 6. Three attackers were charged with murder.[45]

Murders in 1993

Ali Ibrahim, twenty-one years old, a Sudanese asylum seeker, was stabbed in the heart by a drunken man in Brighton on November 7. The judge considered the racial motivation an aggravating factor and sentenced the man to a minimum of twenty years of imprisonment.[46]

Stephen Lawrence, eighteen years old, was attacked and killed by four to six youths on April 22 while waiting for a bus. The gang surrounded him and stabbed him several times. His was the fourth racist murder near the headquarters of the BNP since the establishment of those headquarters in 1992. Two gang members were charged with murder, but the case was dropped for insufficient

---

[45] Peter Rose, "Shopkeeper is left for dead after race attack," *Daily Mail,* November 29, 1994; "Race attack: Five in court," *Daily Mail,* November 30, 1994; Brendan Berry, "Five in Court After Attack on Asian Shopkeeper," *Press Association Newsfile,* November 29, 1994; Paul Stokes, "Asian trader is beaten unconscious ," The *Daily Telegraph,* November 29, 1994; Edward Pilkington And Tony Heath, "Race Attack Shopkeeper Fights for Life," *The Guardian,* November 29, 1994, and Giancarlo Pimpinella, *Most Severe Racially Motivated Attacks* (London: Commission for Racial Equality, 1995).

[46]Clare Dyer, "Judges Urge New Sentence Regime for Murderers," *The Guardian,* April 11, 1995; Richard Ford, "Judges unable to cut killer's 'excessive' 20-year term," *The Times,* April 11, 1995, and Pimpinella, "Most Severe Racially Motivated Attacks."

evidence. The reasons for this lack of evidence are the focus of heated debate. A white youth who witnessed the killing made a statement to the police, but refused to identify anyone for fear of retribution.[47] More significantly, a friend of Stephen's who was also chased during the attack was taken before an identification parade or line-up and identified two of the attackers. His testimony was later considered inadmissible after a police officer filed a statement raising questions about its validity. The boy refuted the officer's claims.[48] The case has been taken up by private prosecution and four men have been charged with murder.[49]

Fiaz Mirza, forty-four years old, was severely beaten, robbed, and locked in the trunk of his car by two white men in February 1993. Mr. Mirza was able to escape from the trunk and run a short distance when the two men followed him, dragged him back, and beat him again. They then threw him off the docks into the water. He suffered brain damage, broken ribs, and twenty-four other injuries. Eighteen days later his body was found. Two white youths were sentenced to life imprisonment. The racist motive was considered an aggravating factor.[50]

Murders in 1992

Panchadcharan Sahitharan, twenty-eight years old, was attacked along with seven other Asians by a gang of white men with baseball bats in Manor Park, east London. He died five days later on January 2, 1992. Gary Hoskin, twenty-one years old, and Andrew Noble, thirty-seven years old, were charged with murder. Gary Hoskin was acquitted on November 3, 1992. [51]

Mohammed Siddiq Dada, sixty years old, was beaten by Wayne Lambert, twenty-five years old, and two accomplices using machetes on January 23, 1992. One of his attackers hit Mr. Dada over the head with an eighteen-inch

---

[47] Pimpinella, "Most Severe Racially Motivated Attacks."

[48] *Private Eye*, May 6, 1994; Human Rights Watch/Helsinki interview with Dev Berrah of Greenwich Action Committee Against Racial Attacks, June 30, 1995; Human Rights Watch/Helsinki interview with J. Deighton of Deighton and Guellera, London, July 3, 1995.

[49] *The Guardian*, April 22, 1995.

[50] Ben Fenton, "Laughing race killers are jailed for life ," *The Daily Telegraph*, September 25, 1993.

[51] Duncan Campbell, "MPs to Call for Legislation on Race Crimes," *The Guardian*, November 9, 1992; "Man Acquitted of Race Murder," *The Guardian*, November 4, 1992.; Pimpinella, "Most Severe Racially Motivated Attacks."

pipe. He was found unconscious in a pool of blood with multiple, deep skull fractures. Mr. Dada died in the hospital on February 5.[52]

Mohammed Sarwar Ansari was attacked three days later, by the same Mr. Lambert and an accomplice, Dean Millington, seventeen years old. They dragged him out of his car and beat him to death. A witness at the trial said that one of the attackers commanded the other to, "finish the Paki off."[53] Mr. Lambert was sentenced to two life sentences for the murders of Mohammed Siddiq Dada and Mohammed Sarwar Ansari. The judge recommended that he should serve a minimum of twenty-five years of imprisonment. Mr. Millington was convicted of the murder of Mohammed Sarwar Ansari and sentenced to be detained indefinitely at Her Majesty's pleasure. The two accomplices in the attack on Mr. Dada were found guilty of manslaughter and sentenced to twelve and thirteen years of imprisonment. The police were initially circumspect about the racial motivation behind these murders, but at the sentencing, Justice Morland told Mr. Lambert: "You were driven by an evil, senseless, barbaric and glaring hatred of Pakistanis."[54]

Navid Sadiq, fifteen years old, was shot in the stomach and temple by Joseph Conroy, twenty-seven years old, on January 25, 1992. Mr. Conroy was given two life sentences for the murder of Mr. Sadiq and the attempted murder of his uncle, Nassar Ali, twenty-five years old. After shooting the two, it was reported

---

[52] Home Affairs Committee, *3rd Report*, p. 174; David Ward, "Families Tell of Ruined Lives and Lost Faith in the Law," *The Guardian*, February 20, 1993; Human Rights Watch/Helsinki interview with Muktar Dar, Manchester, June 29, 1995.

[53] Human Rights Watch/Helsinki interview with Muktar Dar, Manchester, June 29, 1995; Pimpinella , "Most Severe Racially Motivated Attacks." For both of these incidents the police said publicly that the murders were not racist. According to the Manchester Council for Community Relations statement to the Home Affairs Committee: "In a meeting before the trial with the detective who had investigated the two 1992 murders, MCCR learned that *the police knew full well from the day of his arrest that the leader of the murder gang in both cases was a self-confessed racist who hated Pakistanis to an exceptional degree, and the trial made this even clearer.* We explained that the communities affected by racial harassment feel that the police press statements denying or playing down racism when crimes are committed against *black people feel that the police are trying to deny their experience, their problems and their honesty, and that this is felt as an insult."* [Italics in original.]

[54]David Ward, "Families Tell of Ruined Lives and Lost Faith in the Law", *The Guardian*, February 20, 1993; Human Rights Watch/Helsinki interview with Muktar Dar, Manchester, June 29, 1995.

that he stood to attention with his hand in the air and shouted, "Sieg Heil!" Upon arrest he reportedly told the police, "What am I going to get for doing a couple of Pakis?" and regarding his victims said, "I hope they die."[55]

Rohit Duggal, sixteen years old, was stabbed to death on July 11, 1992, after being accosted by two white boys. One of the boys was charged with murder. It was not discovered that the second boy was present until later, but no investigation has taken place regarding his involvement.[56]

Ruhullah Aramesh, twenty-four years old, an Afghan refugee was attacked in Thornton Heath on July 31, 1992, by a gang of twenty yelling racist epithets. They beat him with iron bars and wood planks until his skull was crushed.[57] He died on August 2, 1992. Barry Hannon, seventeen years old, his brother, Paul Hannon, eighteen years old, and Joseph Curtin, seventeen years old, were sentenced to life for murder. Richard Turner, nineteen years old, and Jamie Ware, nineteen years old, were acquitted of manslaughter and murder. Another boy, seventeen years old, whose name was not released, was acquitted for attacking Mr. Aramesh but convicted for assault for having previously attacked a friend of Mr. Aramesh. Barry Hannon and Joseph Curtin had also attacked an Asian family only an hour before killing Mr. Aramesh, hitting a man, sixty-five years old, on the head with a bottle.[58]

Ashiq Hussain, twenty years old, was stabbed to death in the stomach by three drunken white men in Birmingham on September 1. Despite clear directives to the Crown Prosecution Service (CPS) that racist motives should be considered and perhaps taken as an aggravating factor, the prosecution barrister did not appear

---

[55] Duncan Campbell, "MPs to Call for Legislation on Race Crimes," *The Guardian*, November 9, 1992; "Robber Who Shot Dead Boy, 15, is Given Two Life Sentences," *The Guardian*, November 3, 1992; "Life Sentence for 'Nazi Salute' Murder," *Press Association Newsfile*, November 2, 1992; John Steele, "Shot boy thought gun was a fake," *The Daily Telegraph*, October 30, 1993; Pimpinella, "Most Severe Racially Motivated Attacks."

[56] Pimpinella, "Most Severe Racially Motivated Attacks;" Human Rights Watch/Helsinki interview with Dev Berrah of GACARA, June 30, 1995.

[57] David Pallister and Vivek Chaudhary, "Killer Attacks Detective at Old Bailey," *The Guardian*, November 19, 1993; Vivek Chaudhary, "White Gang 'Beat Afghan to Death," *The Guardian*, October 5, 1993.

[58] Duncan Campbell, "MPs to Call for Legislation on Race Crimes," *The Guardian*, November 9, 1992; Heather Mills, "Killer in court outburst at police ," *The Independent*, November 19, 1993.

to acknowledge testimony about the perpetrator's history of racist behavior. The attacker, Mark Jarvis, was out on bail from a twelve-year prison sentence for armed robbery and was described by a senior prison officer as having a history of bullying and racism. A senior security officer also said that Jarvis had attacked an Asian inmate in 1985. Mark Jarvis was accused of murder, found guilty of manslaughter and sentenced to five years.[59]

Aziz Mia, sixty-six years old, was on his way to the local mosque when he was attacked by a white man. He died in the hospital three weeks later as a result of the injuries. The attacker was sentenced to life imprisonment for murder.

Murders in 1991

Orville Blair, twenty-five years old, was stabbed to death by a white man living on his estate. White gangs calling themselves Nazi Turnouts reportedly were roaming the streets chanting "two nil" referring to Mr. Blair and the murder of Roland Adams three months earlier.[60]

Roland Adams, fifteen years old, was attacked by a gang of fifteen white youths in February 1991. He died as a result of being stabbed in the neck. Roland's father Richard Adams said: "After his death, we received abusive phone calls, up to ten times a night. In the end, we were forced to move."[61]

---

[59]Pail Myers, "Prisoner on Home Leave Killed Asian," *The Guardian*, July 7, 1993; "Asian driver is stabbed to death," *The Independent*, September 3, 1992; "Taxi Driver Stabbed to Death," *The Guardian*, September 3, 1992; Mervyn Tunbridge, "Police Hunt Taxi Driver's Killers," *Press Association Newsfile*, September 21, 1992; Home Affairs Committee, 3rd Report: Racial Attacks and Harassment, Vol. 1, 1994, p. 107; Human Rights Watch/Helsinki interview with Vicram Dodd, June 6, 1995.

[60] Mark Honigsbaum, "The New Racist Fears on London's Streets," *Evening Standard*, May 24, 1993; Paul Harris, Peter Rose, "How Race Militants Hijacked a Tragedy," *Daily Mail*, May 10, 1993.

[61] *Irish Times*, March 8, 1993.

4. RACIALLY MOTIVATED VIOLENCE

Incidents of racist violence that do not result in murder range from vicious and brutal assaults to harassment. All incidents are deeply troubling to the victims and further destabilize the sense of security in local communities. Below is a brief list of significant cases that captured the attention of the British media.[62]

Quddus Ali was attacked on September 8, 1993, on Commercial Road in London by a gang of white men and one woman. They kicked and beat him to the ground. While he was lying in the gutter, they repeatedly kicked his head against the curb. After the attack he was in a coma for several months and still suffers from severe brain damage. Five people were arrested. One was accused of attempted murder, but was acquitted.[63]

Mukhtar Ahmed, nineteen years old, and five friends were walking on Bethnal Green Road in London, February 8, 1994, when they were attacked and chased by twenty white youths who came at them from two directions. The attack was clearly planned. While his friends were able to escape, Muktar was chased to a dead end. According to the prosecution, John Hardy, "He was punched to the floor. He curled up in a ball to protect himself as best he could. His head was kicked backwards and forwards as though it was some sort of football in a school playground. He was soon unconscious. His facial appearance was grotesque to the point of being unrecognizable."[64] Muktar was beaten mostly about the head with staves and kicked. During the attack, the perpetrators chanted, "Paki!" He received forty-eight stitches crisscrossing his face and scalp and suffered a broken jaw. He was in a coma for several days.

Nicky Fuller, seventeen years old, was found guilty of the attack on Muktar Ahmed. He was sentenced to only six months in prison and then immediately released because he had already served six months while on remand.

---

[62] All of the victims in the cases below are members of ethnic minorities; information about these cases and contact with the victims was provided or facilitated by support groups for victims of racist violence.

[63] "End Race War, Begs Coma Boy's Mother," *Daily Mail*, September 13, 1993; Maurice Chittenden and Rajeev Syal, "Race-attack gangs fuel fears of street wars ," *Sunday Times*, September 12, 1993; Chris Brooke and Peter Rose, "Violence erupts at hospital race vigil; Race attack vigil ends in violence," *Daily Mail*, September 11, 1993; Shekhar Bhatia, "Language of Hate that has Left My Son Close to Death," *Evening Standard*, September 10, 1993; Pimpinella, "Most Severe Racially Motivated Attacks."

[64] "Girlfriend Turned in Race Attack Youth," *The Guardian*, October 27, 1994.

Judge Peter Rountree said that Mr. Fuller had played only a peripheral role in the attack, but noted that under the Criminal Justice Bill, which was to go into effect the next year, Mr. Fuller could have been sentenced to two years.

Mr. Fuller's girlfriend, Kelly Turner, was a principal witness in the case. She had kept detailed diaries of conversations with Mr. Fuller regarding the attack and the names of those involved. An excerpt is quoted from a statement she made to the press:

> One of Nicky's friends phoned and said: "I've been in the nick all day. We beat a Paki boy up last night and we're going to be done for attempted murder." The next day, Nicky phoned three times before I got back from school. When I spoke to him, he told me: "We did a Paki." He wanted to go back out with me. He was trying to impress me, act macho. At first I thought they were making it up, but then I saw the news and everything he'd just told me came up on the telly. The police appealed for anyone with information to come forward. After that, I kept notes of all the telephone conversations I had with them and names they mentioned. I went back to Hollywoods the next week after the attack, before I'd made my statement. I saw Nicky again and I asked him what had happened. He said: "There was loads of us. We all put in a couple of boots. I've got that Paki boy's blood on my trainers [sneakers]." He had white Reebok trainers with a gray strip, really dirty and horrible, and he had blood in that bit where the laces are. It was all congealed. He'd left it on his trainers, he was obviously proud of it being there. He told me that they were planning to kill Muktar, or cripple him. They only stopped kicking him when a woman living in the flats nearby came out and shouted at them. They ran off and she cradled Muktar in her arms and talked to him until the police came. It took five hours to talk my statement through with the police, and five hours to write it up.
>
> ...Nicky was arrested and taken to a council safe house. Then the calls started...before I had to appear in court, we got threatening calls every half hour right through the night...One of Nicky's friends, the one who followed me, was tried with him, but he walked free. They didn't have enough evidence. There's been a series of attacks on Asians in that area and the police told us they

are 99 percent sure the same boys were involved in those...There were other people who could have come forward if they had wanted to, but they were too scared...When I first told one of my teachers about the phone calls, he said: "Well, I don't want you in the school because my other pupils will be at risk if these people come after you." The school's attitude towards the bullying was, if you don't like it, you can leave...Even a friend of my dad's said to me: "You want to keep quiet. Don't stick up for those black bastards because you'll get a brick through your window...I still feel nervous about going down Barking or Bow without my mum...when I'm walking home, I'm always looking back.[65]

Prosecutor John Hardy told the court, "Others bear greater responsibility for the ferocity of the attack...they have yet to be brought to justice."[66]

Mr. Fuller pleaded not guilty to an initial allegation of causing grievous bodily harm with intent. This plea was accepted for lack of evidence. Anthony Peak, eighteen years old, was found not guilty of both charges of causing grievous bodily harm with intent and violent disorder. The police claimed that there was a "conspiracy of silence" among the white community that prevented an effective case being brought against the other attackers. The fact that no one else was charged is the source of some controversy and is discussed later.

Chadik Miah, fourteen years old, was ambushed and beaten around the head by ten white men a few hours before the attack on Mr. Ahmed.[67]

Students from the Tower Hamlets college were attacked two days after the assault on Mr. Miah by men armed with baseball bats and garden tools. The attacks on these students, Chadik and Mukhtar, were part of a series of nine total attacks that appeared to have been planned by adults. All of these incidents occurred in the East End of London. Other incidents included a man being dragged

---

[65] Emma Brooker, "Witness," *The Guardian*, November 7, 1994.

[66] Sean O'Neill, "Silence thwarts attack inquiry," *The Daily Telegraph*, October 27, 1994. See also Vivek Chaudhary, "Call for Race Violence Law as Attacker is Freed," *The Guardian*, November 16, 1994; Melvyn Howe , "Youth in Race Scalping Attack Walks Free," *Press Association Newsfile*, November 15, 1994; Human Rights Watch/Helsinki interview with Ranjit Lohia of the Community Association for Police Accountability (CAPA), London, March 14, 1995.

[67]"Racist Wave Sweeps East End," *The Observer*, February 13, 1994.

from his car and assaulted and boys beaten and stabbed on their way home from school.[68]

Shah Allem, seventeen years old, and **Shahid Uddin**, twenty-six years old, were attacked on May 30. Ten white skinheads crossed the street to confront them. Shahid ran and was pursued by three youths who beat him with a baseball bat. Shah was slashed with a knife, suffering deep wounds to his lung and kidney and other areas of his body. He was hit on the head with a hammer and collapsed to the ground. One young man was charged with actual bodily harm on Shahid, another was charged in connection with Shah's injuries. Two other youths were later arrested.[69]

Clive Forbes, thirty-seven years old, was assaulted by ten white men on June 13, 1993. They beat him with a metal bar. He managed to escape and barricade himself in his home, but the two men smashed down his door, caught him and continued to beat and kick him, and clubbed his head with an iron bar. He leapt twenty-five feet from a balcony to escape and broke his leg as a result of the fall. He was hospitalized for seven weeks. Jason Craney, twenty-one years old, and Paul Corbet, twenty-five years old, were sentenced to thirteen years for grievous bodily harm. A charge of attempted murder was dropped. The racial motivation was an aggravating factor in the sentence.[70]

Attacks By Neighbors

Afro-Caribbean and Asian families are often terrorized by campaigns of violence from white neighbors and their friends. The victims are not only frequently attacked, but often by the people they see on a daily basis next door or

---

[68]"Assaults Spark Fear of London Race War," *The Observer*, February 13, 1994; "Racist Wave Sweeps East End," *The Observer*, February 13, 1994.

[69] Human Rights Watch/Helsinki interview with Deb Dey, Tower Hamlets Law Center, June 5, 1995; Pimpinella, "Most Severe Racially Motivated Attacks."

[70]Ian Burrell, "Racist gangs drive out black families," *Sunday Times*, September 17, 1995; "Years for Race Attack, Thugs Who Attacked Clive Forbes Jailed," *Daily Mirror*, November 10, 1994; "Jail for race attack," *The Independent*, November 10, 1994; Richard Ford, "Race-attack victim is critical," *The Times*, June 16, 1993; Heather Mills, "Racism in Europe: Britain: Law helps contain violence,"*The Independent*, June 18, 1993; Pimpinella, "Most Severe Racially Motivated Attacks."

in their community. These attacks are explicit efforts by members of white communities to force ethnic minorities out of their homes.[71]

Interviews conducted by Human Rights Watch/Helsinki indicate that many Afro-Caribbean and Asian families face ongoing racist violence and harassment sometimes for years in and around their homes. During these campaigns, white neighbors smash their windows, set fire to their letter boxes, smear feces around the entrance of their homes, spit on them as they leave their home, assault parents and children, and spray paint graffiti demanding that they leave the country.

If these campaigns are to be stopped, decisive action must be taken by local authorities. Unfortunately there are too many reports of lax or even hostile responses by the authorities to families who suffer daily from such abuse. In addition, the current law is too weak to be effective in situations where the violence is less severe, but the abuse and harassment occur frequently. In many cases the police do not respond because they simply do not consider a broken window, graffiti, or a victim being punched, sufficiently serious to invest time and money in a thorough investigation.

Taken on a case by case basis, each physical attack or act of vandalism may appear to the police as comparatively minor in nature. When viewed as an organized campaign of violence and harassment, however, it can be devastating to a neighborhood. Current police practice and law are not effective at curtailing coordinated racist attacks that in isolation are not severe, but as a whole are very damaging. As a result, numerous families are regularly victimized and left unprotected, while the perpetrators are not investigated or charged. This dynamic undermines trust in the police and the legal system, causing ethnic minorities to doubt these institutions' ability to protect them from crimes systematically perpetrated against them.

Ms. F. has faced ongoing racially motivated violence and harassment since 1992. On March 16, 1993, a stone was thrown through Ms. F.'s window. On March 18, 1993, Ms. F. was attacked by a white man who punched her, grabbed her by the throat and banged her head against the wall. She suffered bruising to her throat and head.[72]

---

[71] These efforts violate the Universal Declaration of Human Rights, including Art. 13:1. Everyone has the right to freedom of movement and residence within the borders of each state.

[72] Written testimony from Ms. F submitted to Human Rights Watch/Helsinki; Internal reports from community groups and agencies.

She is regularly spat on, verbally abused, and threatened by neighbors who say they will "get" her. Objects are regularly thrown at her as she approaches her home. On February 20, 1993, an object was thrown hitting her on the back of the head, followed by someone yelling, "Black cunt, watch what's gonna happen to you. I'm watching you." On February 28, an object hit her three-year-old daughter in the face. People in her estate bang on her front door and yell, "down with all blacks, you're not wanted here, the nigger's children gonna get bashed, the kids will die." Between February 19 and March 2, 1993, Ms. F. was harassed on sixteen separate occasions.[73]

Daniel:

Trouble started from the beginning when we moved in 1991. It began when our upstairs neighbors were building and banging around which was doing damage to our ceiling. We brought them down to show them what was happening. One of them slapped my wife and called her "Nigger lover." They said they would run her out of the area. From then on the incidents increased. They would make threats as we would leave the house, saying "I'm going to kill you" or "I'm going to blow your fucking head off." They made it clear that they wanted to get us out. The windows of our car were broken twice.

Another time when I opened my door they were standing there and yelled that they were going to teach me a lesson. They said, "You fuckin' nigger, we are going to kill you, you should not be in this country." One of the men lunged at me with a crowbar. I protected myself with my hand, but he smashed my knuckles. My wife called the police, but when they came they said they could not do anything because there were no independent witnesses.

I came home once from work in February 1994. There had been a break-in. Only a few small items had been stolen, but not valuable ones. There was graffiti spray painted in my kitchen: "You black bastard go home, Black bastard, You white slut."

---

[73] Case history and testimony submitted to Human Rights Watch/Helsinki, June 27, 1995.

During the same month my wife opened the door and found the neighbor's rubbish at our front door. She put it back in front of their door. Then there was a knock at our door. There were two women there. They said they wanted me to start collecting their rubbish. I said no. One of them went crazy. She kicked me in the groin. I wanted to hit back, but had the feeling it was a trap. If I would respond, then they would really get me. She kicked me three times. She kicked the rubbish into the room. A plastic bottle hit my daughter in the head. One of the women ran into our room and grabbed my wife, "you nigger lover," and pushed her back. She [Daniel's wife] later went to the hospital for internal bleeding. I tried to push the lady out.

My wife called the police. When they came they spoke to the white family and then said *to us*, "In view of what I have seen I'm placing you under arrest for assault." The woman said I hit her in the nose. There was no blood around. They were arresting us, but we called them for help. They took me into a cell and did not let me out for hours. They did not question us about what happened until the next day. The police spoke to them, but it seemed very polite, but they put me in a cell.

A few months later we found rubbish in front of our door again. This time I called the police straight away. I did not want trouble. They came and I showed them the rubbish bag. The woman came and attacked me in front of the police. I said, "This is what happens when you are here. Imagine what happens when you are not." They arrested her, but let her out within thirty minutes. I have given up on the police even though the harassment continues.

Another time, two guys threatened my wife with a knife and said that if we got others involved in the situation they would kill the kids. They knew which school the kids went to and knew where my wife worked.[74]

---

[74] Human Rights Watch/Helsinki interview with victims, Brighton, June 17, 1995.

Sandra:

The trouble started as soon as we moved into that area in 1991. We would get excrement through the door. Parents put nails through planks of wood and gave them to their children to hit our children. In 1993, two guys came into our house and beat up John badly. The police did not come for hours. When you realize that anyone can come into your house, you become terrified. The police would just say, "don't push further it will make things worse" or "it [the situation] will defuse over time." We found the fluid for our brakes was drained out.

Once when we arrived home we saw thirty people standing around. Some were our neighbors, but they must have brought people from outside. One said, "We want you out, we will get you out, I'm bringing the boys." They were all screaming. It was horrible. Eventually the police came. The crowd fell silent, moved aside a bit to their own doorways. The police did not question anyone or say anything to them.

After we made complaints to the police we started getting harassed by the police. They would stop John and search him all the time. He has never done anything wrong. They never find anything. It all blends together.[75]

Mohammed:

Everyone in this house has been beaten by them [the neighbors]. Every time we go out of the house we get spit at and pushed. They yell at us, "Paki shit, go home." They come to our house and kick the door. They smear shit on the door. They smashed the kitchen window. We are fed up. We need peace. During the BNP campaign the young white lads would come around and say to our children, "you are taking our country." Our children get chased to school and when they come home. Now our children go to school at 8:30 a.m. to avoid the white boys and a teacher brings them home. We call the police often, but they come very

---

[75] Human Rights Watch/Helsinki interview, Manchester, June 28, 1995. Documents received by Human Rights Watch Helsinki, June 28, 1995.

late after the white lads are gone and the police can't find them. We do not feel free. We are not safe to leave our house.[76]

---

[76] Human Rights Watch/Helsinki interview, London, July 4, 1995.

5. THE ROLE OF THE POLICE

Reports to Human Rights Watch/Helsinki indicate that the police are often unable or unwilling to respond effectively to racist violence. Most shocking are the number of reports of vicious and racist treatment at the hands of the police themselves.

Deaths in Police Custody

A number of deaths have been reported in police custody, indicating that officers are inappropriately trained or in some cases engaging in racially motivated police brutality. Because Afro-Caribbeans and Asians communities feel generally mistreated and at times victimized by the police, reports of deaths in police custody increase the level of fear and mistrust regardless of the actual cause.

The degree to which each death is the result of racial bias, poor training, or a combination of the two is very difficult to determine accurately in every case. Members of the ethnic minority communities expressed deep concern about the numbers of individuals, especially African and African-Caribbeans, who die under suspicious circumstances while in police custody. Helen Shaw, of Inquest, pointed to the failure to prosecute the responsible police as an important factor[77]:

> To date there has only been one prosecution of a police officer involved in a death in custody case. Even in cases where there has been an inquest verdict of unlawful killing, the Crown Prosecution Service (CPS) has thrown the case out, usually on grounds of insufficient evidence. Inquest feels that the CPS, in such cases, should at least allow the case to go to trial.[78]

This failure to act suggests to victims that there is systematic racial bias and aggressive or violent behavior by police against such groups which lead to disproportionately more deaths. According to interviews with victims and their solicitors, there remains significant doubt that these cases are handled effectively.

---

[77] Inquest monitors and provides legal assistance in cases involving deaths in police custody.

[78] Interview with Helen Shaw, Inquest, by Human Rights Watch/Helsinki, October 16, 1996.

A report by the United Nations Committee on the Elimination of Racial Discrimination, given on March 14, 1996, stated, "It is noted with serious concern that among the victims of death in custody are a disproportionate number of members of minority groups, that police brutality appears to affect members of minority groups disproportionately, that allegations of police brutality and harassment are reportedly not vigorously investigated and perpetrators, once guilt is established, not appropriately punished."[79]

Below are many of the cases that have raised concern that police misconduct is directed primarily at ethnic minorities, and that the current procedures for investigating these cases do not result in offending officers being held accountable for their misconduct.

Joy Gardner, forty years old, died on August 1, 1993, after immigration officers attempted to deport her. The circumstances behind the deportation order, the behavior of the officers and the equipment used that led to her death raised many serious questions.

When the officers arrived at her home on July 28, Mrs. Gardner had not yet received notification that her application to gain permanent residency had been rejected. Her lawyers received two letters from the Home Office rejecting her case on the day the officers arrived to deport her. These letters were dated July 26 and 27, 1993. As a result, Mrs. Gardner was surprised by the deportation team that arrived prepared for a violent confrontation.[80]

Mrs. Gardner allegedly refused to allow the team to enter her home. When the officers forced their way in, Mrs. Gardner reportedly became violent. One officer unplugged the telephone to prevent her from contacting her lawyer. Several officers cuffed her and forced her down to the floor. Two officers held her legs and one officer sat on her midsection.

Another officer placed a body-belt around her waist, bound her wrists to handcuffs attached to the belt, and tied her thighs and ankles with leather belts. He then wrapped two rolls of adhesive tape totaling thirteen feet around her head. He testified that this was done to prevent her from biting him while he was trying to hold her head still. He also testified that the second roll was used because she was

---

[79] "UN Race Group Raps 'Police Brutality,'" Andrew Woodcock, Press Association Newsfile, March 15, 1996.

[80] Three members from the Alien Deportation Group (ADG) accompanied an immigration official. At the time, the ADG was used in cases where resistance from deportees was expected. According to officials, Mrs. Gardner had two prior restraining orders against her by her husband and therefore might resist deportation. The ADG was disbanded after her death in August 1993.

"biting the tape" and was able to pull the gag from the first roll. However, according to testimony from other officers her arms were already fastened to the body belt making this impossible. Additionally, according to Dr. Harris from the Forensic Science Service at Huntington Laboratories who examined the tape, there were no teeth marks on the tape.

Shortly after the tape was applied Mrs. Gardner stopped moving. An ambulance was called and arrived at 8:15 a.m., but the emergency medical team discovered her heart had stopped. She was pronounced dead at the hospital. Initially, the Home Office claimed the death was due to kidney failure, but later said that she had died from head injuries received during the struggle. Numerous other autopsy reports and post-mortem examinations, however, indicated that she suffered brain damage due to oxygen deprivation, and that the tape gag was the principal cause of death.

Ten years before this incident, in 1983, Metropolitan Police lawyers instructed, "it would be very difficult to justify gagging a deportee when not in flight on an aircraft." The gag is not referred to in the Police Self-Defense & Restraint Manual and a former ADG officer said that officers taught themselves how to use them. While the use of restraint must be recorded in other circumstances by police officers, there were no requirements for the deportation squad to do so. Although gags had been used a number of times before Mrs. Gardner's death, medical risks were never considered. Dr. Iain West testified at the trial that "the use of a gag is dangerous... and may often result in... serious harm because [the] airway may be obstructed in a number of ways. Sometimes the effect is to completely close off the air passage." The ADG officers involved were tried for manslaughter and acquitted between May 15 and June 14, 1995. They faced no disciplinary action.

Since the death of Mrs. Gardner a number of important changes have been made: The use of the mouth-gag was appropriately suspended by the Commissioner of the Metropolitan Police in August 1993 and banned by the Home Secretary in January 1994; arm and leg restraints can now only be used before boarding an aircraft; training with restraint equipment is more rigorous, as is first-aid training specific to restraint equipment; police assistance in deportation efforts must be requested through a more detailed process; the deportee will not be removed from the country on the day he/she is arrested for deportation, except

under "exceptional circumstances;"[81] planning sessions will be required when
violence is expected in deportation efforts.[82]

Oliver Pryce, thirty years old. On July 24, 1990, at about 9:30 p.m. Mr.
Pryce, suffering from a mental breakdown, threw himself in front of an oncoming
ambulance. Six officers arrived and grabbed him as he continued stumbling on the
road. One officer seized Mr. Pryce in a necklock and put him into the van face
down. Another officer lay over his shoulders while more officers sat on his arms
and legs. Mr. Pryce remained pinned to the floor until the van arrived at the police
station. Witnesses reportedly said they feared that he had been choked at the time
of arrest because they saw his body "spasm" before it went limp. Witnesses also
said that he did not appear to be struggling with the police during the arrest. Police
claimed that he stopped moving only once they arrived at the station. Cardiologist
Dr. Adrian Davis testified later that he most likely died in the police van. He was
declared dead at Middlesbrough General Hospital at 10:25 p.m. It was determined
that he had died of asphyxiation. In contrast to witness reports saying that he did
not struggle, officers described Mr. Pryce as a "wild animal" and "drug-crazed."

Before an inquest had been completed the Director of Public Prosecutions
(DPP) announced that the officers would not be prosecuted. In November 1991, an
inquest jury found that he had been "unlawfully killed." This finding forced the
DPP to reconsider, but he finally ruled that no disciplinary measures should be
taken against the officers. This ruling was shortly seconded by the Police
Complaints Authority (PCA). A spokesman for the PCA said that there was
insufficient evidence to prove beyond reasonable doubt that the police officers
committed a disciplinary offense of abuse of authority. The family of Mr. Pryce
filed a suit against the Cleveland Constabulary for assault, battery and negligence.

Eventually, four years after the verdict, the Cleveland Constabulary
accepted liability for the death of Oliver Pryce and paid damages to the family.
Despite this admission of responsibility, no disciplinary action has been taken
against the officers involved and the Cleveland Constabulary indicated that no
action will be taken. The Association of Chief Police Officers eventually

---

[81] This term is left vague. *The Independent*, August 21, 1996.

[82] Compiled from Amnesty International, *United Kingdom—Death in Policy
Custody of Joy Gardner*, (London: Amnesty International, August 1995); documents
submitted to Human Rights Watch/Helsinki from Inquest; Human Rights Watch/Helsinki
interview with Deborah Coles from Inquest, London, January 15, 1996.

distributed a notice to all chief constables indicating that neckholds should be "avoided if at all possible."[83]

Following this case, the Police Complaints Authority notified all forces that, "A neck hold which exerts any pressure on the carotid artery or which compresses the airway involves, except in extreme circumstances, an unacceptably high element of risk."[84]

Leon Patterson, thirty-two years old, was found dead, naked, and covered with bruises in his Denton, Greater Manchester, prison cell on November 27, 1992, at 1:20 a.m. On November 23, 1992, he had been taken to a doctor for treatment for repeated vomiting. The prison cleaner later testified that he had to remove eight blankets from the cell because they were stained with vomit, and that Mr. Patterson was lying on the floor muttering to himself. The following day the cleaner found blood smeared on the walls, green slime on the floor, and green balls in the lavatory bowl. He said that Mr. Patterson was naked, rolling on the floor and incoherent. According to reports, he was left for more than twenty hours suffering from seizures and fits of vomiting that covered the walls with blood.

Despite his condition, police doctors felt that he was fit enough to attend his scheduled court appearance. He was carried, naked and handcuffed, to the courtroom cells. Police admitted later that they believed he was faking his illness. He was visited there by a doctor at 7 p.m. who determined that he was mentally ill, but found no physical symptoms and determined that he was fit for detention overnight. It was later learned that Mr. Patterson was suffering from extreme dehydration after eating and drinking little, and repeatedly vomiting. At 9 p.m. he

---

[83] Nick Cohen, "Man unlawfully killed in back of police van," *The Independent*, November 30, 1991; Nick Cohen, "PC denies using excessive force"; *The Independent*, November 27, 1991; Nick Cohen, "Arrested man was like raging bull, PC tells inquest,"*The Independent*, November 26, 1991; Heather Mills, "Family of custody victim wages fight for justice," *The Independent*, August 12, 1993; "Police Involved in Death Arrest Will not Face Discipline Charges," *The Guardian*, July 29, 1992; "Police 'killed karate expert'," *The Daily Telegraph*, November 30, 1991; "Bar asked to act on death in custody," *The Daily Telegraph*, November 3, 1992; Clare Dyer, "Black Lawyers Attack Bar Over Death in Police Custody Inquiry," *The Guardian*, January 25, 1993; Heather Mills, "Family angered by CPS refusal to prosecute," *The Independent*, March 27, 1995; *Home Affairs Committee, 3rd Report: Racial Attacks and Harassment*, Vol. 1, 1994, p. 174; Human Rights Watch/Helsinki interview with Deborah Coles, Inquest, London, January 16, 1996.

[84]Owen Bowcott, "Jail Death Raises Neck Hold Fears," *The Guardian,* February 3, 1996.

stopped moaning. At 1:20 a.m. he stopped breathing. He was later found dead in the cell with bruises covering his body.

His body was initially examined by Dr. John Rutherford, and tissue samples were studied by Mr. Richardson of Manchester Royal Infirmary. Based on their analyses, Dr. Rutherford said Mr. Patterson died of an overdose of nitrazepam. Mr. Patterson commissioned an independent analysis from Dr. Sheila Dawling of the National Prison Unit who found no traces of nitrazepam. When the data of Mr. Rutherford's analysis was requested and he was cross-examined in court, he confessed that he panicked and faked the results using samples taken from another body, but maintained his belief in the cause of death. Dr. Dawling testified that an overdose of nitrazepam usually results in coma, not violent delirium, and is almost never fatal.

The first inquest into his death was adjourned when it was learned that a member of the jury was the wife of a serving officer in the Greater Manchester Police. The second inquest in March 1993 investigating the conduct of several police officers and three police surgeons determined that Mr. Patterson was unlawfully killed as a result of "reckless" lack of care for having failed to send him to the hospital. The verdict was challenged by eight police officers and three police surgeons. Mr. Justice Ognall approved a "statement of compromise" which called for a new hearing due to confusion regarding the distinction between lack of care and unlawful killing. On November 25, 1996, the third inquest found that Mr.

Patterson's death was the result of "misadventure to which neglect contributed."[85]

Shiji Lapite, thirty years old, was stopped by two plainclothes police officers, PC Paul Wright, twenty-eight years old, and Andrew McCallum, twenty-four years old, from Stoke Newington for "acting suspiciously" just after midnight on December 16, 1994. During the arrest, the police officers claim Lapite resisted violently. He died in the police van on the way to the station.

The officers claimed that they had seen Lapite drop two cling-film wrapped rocks of crack cocaine by a tree, and when they went to question him he became violent. One officer claimed that Mr. Lapite suddenly became "the most violent man I have ever come across" and his strength must have been caused by crack cocaine. According to the arresting officer, Mr. Lapite "pretended to be unconscious" and was only taken to the hospital when they realized his condition was more serious.

Both officers admitted kicking Mr. Lapite in the head, biting him and pinning him down with a neck hold, but said they did not use excessive force. They claimed that they were protecting themselves because he was attempting to strangle PC Wright, although a pathologist found no evidence of this on the officer's neck. A Home Office pathologist said that "serious doubt must be thrown on the allegation" for lack of evidence of bruises.

A post-mortem examination determined that Mr. Lapite died of asphyxia in connection with a necklock or strangle hold that crushed his voice box. He also

---

[85]John Aston, "New Inquest Into Cell Death of Naked Prisoner," *Press Association Newsfile*, October 14, 1994; "UK: Police Complaints Authority Complete Supervision of Investigation into Death of Leon Patterson," *Hermes - UK Government Press Releases*, April 12, 1994; David Rose, "UK: Sick, Naked Prisoner was Unlawfully Killed - Home Office Pathologist Admidst he Faked Data," *The Observer*, May 2, 1993; Paul Donovan, "Hidden evidence," *The Independent*, January 15, 1997; Owen Bowcott , "Thief Who Died 'Held Face Down by Four Police'," *The Guardian*, November 26, 1996; Louise Jury, "Police neglect contributed to prisoner's death," *The Independent*, November 26, 1996; John Deane, "Misadventure Verdict on Man Who Died in Police Cell," *Press Association Newsfile*, November 26, 1996; David Ward, "Cell Death Man Beaten'," *The Guardian*, November 5, 1996; "Dead addict 'feigned illness'," *The Independent*, November 5, 1996; "Cell-death error," *The Independent*, November 5, 1996; Peter Beal, "PC Thought Cell Death Man Had Been Faking Illness," *Press Association Newsfile*, November 4, 1996; "UK: Cell-Death Family's Agony," *Manchester Evening News*, November 2, 1996; "UK:Police Complaints Authority and Ethnic Minority Deaths in Custody," *Hermes - UK Government Press Release*, October 29, 1996; Finlay Marshall, "Cell Death Man's Twin Sister Calls for Inquiry," *Press Association Newsfile*, October 29, 1996.

suffered forty-five injuries including bruises and abrasions to the head and face. A later post-mortem also showed that he had taken cocaine and a small amount of alcohol. The CPS said it would not bring charges against the officers involved because there was insufficient evidence for a realistic chance of a successful prosecution. After the CPS declared that there was insufficient evidence, an inquest jury found on January 25, 1996, that Mr. Lapite had been "unlawfully killed" by the officers.

At the end of the inquest hearing the coroner, Stephen Chan, asked the deputy assistant commissioner, Lawrence Roach, to indicate to the Association of Chief Police Officers that "all police officers should be brought up to date with the hazards and dangers of this particular technique...neck holds should, at best, be avoided." The CPS reconsidered the case, but on August 9, 1996, returned with the same decision not to prosecute the officers involved in the incident. Despite the inquest findings the CPS report said, "There is insufficient evidence to ensure any criminal proceedings in connection with the death."

On December 2, 1996, the PCA criticized the police service for failing to instruct its officers properly regarding the dangers of neck holds, but said that no disciplinary action would be taken against the officers. Ms. Molly Meacher stated, "The evidence does not prove that the neck hold which contributed to Shiji Lapite's death represented unnecessary violence; this tragedy highlights the vital need for the police service to ensure that their officers are aware of the dangers of neck holds."[86]

In response to the announcement, Deborah Coles of Inquest told the press, "This decision follows a pattern of cases where officers whose conduct has led to death or serious injury have not been subject to criminal or disciplinary hearings."

A statement by the PCA said that officers may use force if they fear that their own or a colleague's life is at risk and that "it is not possible to prove, beyond a reasonable doubt, that the officers did not fear for their lives. The officers assert that they did."[87]

The PCA said that it was informed that safer methods of restraint were available, and thus deduced that "the officers were not properly trained in available alternative methods of restraint." The statement, however, does not make clear whether it was clearly determined that the officers were unaware of alternative methods. The statement also makes no effort to determine the strength of the

---

[86]"UK: Police Complaints Authority - Death in Custody of Shiji Lapite-Disciplinary Outcome," *Hermes - UK Government Press Releases,* December 2, 1996.

[87]Ibid.

officer's claim that Mr. Lapite attempted to strangle one of the officers in light of the fact that a pathologist found no evidence on his neck.

It is disturbing that in a case involving death in police custody, the officer's claim that Mr. Lapite was attempting to strangle an officer, which was not supported by a pathologist, should be sufficient to cast enough doubt to avoid *any kind* of disciplinary action.

The family's solicitor, Raju Bhatt is reportedly seeking a judicial review in the High Court of the CPS decision not to prosecute the officers and against the PCA for not disciplining them.[88]

Wayne Douglas, twenty-five years old, died on December 5, 1995, after being arrested by several officers. The incident sparked a riot in Brixton. According to *The Guardian*, a witness said that Mr. Douglas was beaten by officers while being arrested and was himself chased away by one of the officers.

According to police records, a couple was robbed at knife point and telephoned the police at 2:36 a.m. They said that Douglas matched the description of the burglar and was seen dropping credit cards. Mr. Douglas was arrested at 2:46 and arrived at the station at 2:58 a.m. Police claim that Mr. Douglas "spoke to officers and was answering coherently." Officers recorded that Mr. Douglas had "blood coming from the mouth." The custody sheet indicated that at 3:31 a.m., Mr. Douglas was making a noise, when an officer went into his cell and found that he had stopped breathing and that "his jaw was locked and his eyes were bulging." He was pronounced dead at the hospital. A post-mortem determined that he died of a heart attack. The Crown Prosecution Service announced on August 5 that no police officer would be prosecuted for the death.

On December 6, 1996, a jury returned a verdict of "accidental death." One post-mortem examination by Frederick Patel indicated that he died from hypertensive heart disease. Bernard Knight concluded, however, that positional

---

[88]Jason Bennetto, "No charges over police van death," *The Independent,* July 19, 1995; "When police have a stranglehold on the truth," *The Independent,* July 3, 1995; Duncan Campbell, "No Charges Over Death In Custody," *The Guardian,* August 10, 1996; Jojo Moyes, "Police cleared on arrest death," *The Independent,* August 10, 1996; Heather Mills, "Police chiefs 'ignore claims of brutality'," *The Independent,* January 27, 1996; Vivek Chaudhary And Owen Bowcott, "Asylum Seeker 'Unlawfully Killed' By Police," *The Guardian,* January 26, 1996; "Family Fury at 'No Action' on Police Who Killed," Duncan Campbell, *The Guardian,* December 3, 1996; "Outrage as police cleared over asylum-seeker's death," Jason Bennetto, *The Independent,* December 3, 1996; "UK: Police Complaints Authority - Death in Custody of Shiji Lapite- Disciplinary Outcome," *Hermes - UK Government Press Releases,* December 2, 1996; Interview with Deborah Coles of Inquest, London, July 18, 1996; Interview with Raju Bhatt, London, July 1995. .

asphyxia was the cause and found no evidence of heart disease. Sir Montague Levine, the coroner, said that he was "appalled" to learn that Metropolitan Police officers received just ten minutes training on the risks of asphyxia caused by suspects being held face down when their hands are handcuffed behind them. [89]

During the inquires, the police claimed that Mr. Douglas violently resisted arrest and lunged at them with a long kitchen knife. [90] PC James Page said that as he and PC Gavin McKay approach Mr. Douglas, Mr. Douglas punched Mr. Page in the face, pulled a knife from his pocket and waved it in the air. "I was terrified," PC Page said, "my fear was that I could get stabbed and die." According to Mr. Page, Mr. Douglas then ran off, throwing the knife to the ground, but then stopped, faced them again, and drew another knife, then turned and ran again.   He periodically stopped, turned, and lunged at the officers with the knife, until he reached the park, when he again turned on the officer. "At this point, I again feared for my life... and I struck him on the left side of the chest," Mr. Page testified. Mr. McKay hit him on the wrist, knocking the knife out of his hand.[91]

Eyewitness Patrick Doyle testified that he heard the police shout "put it down" and then saw a knife thrown to the ground. Two of the officers, according to Mr. Doyle, then rushed Mr. Douglas, "pinned" him to the ground. Mr. Doyle said the police acted like "a pack of hyenas going in for the kill, raining blows on the boy with batons... some of the officers were also stamping on him... on his chest, arms, legs, back, head, everywhere. They were also kicking him... I do not know how many times they hit him." [92]

Another eyewitness, Kenneth Johnson testified, "I heard the words, 'I can't breath, I can't breath'".[93]

---

[89]"Charges will not be pressed ," *The Economist*, August 10, 1996; Duncan Campbell and Owen Bowcott, Baton Death Verdict 'Unjust' Police 'need better training'," *The Guardian*, August 9, 1996; Human Rights Watch/Helsinki interview with Deborah Coles of Inquest, London, January 16, 1996.

[90] Ibid; "Black Burglary Suspect's Death 'Was an Accident'," Sue Clough, *The Daily Telegraph*, December 7, 1996; Human Rights Watch/Helsinki, interview with Helen Shaw, Inquest, London, October 16, 1996.

[91] "Policemen 'in fear for lives' during knife chase," *The Herald (Glasgow)*, November 20, 1996.

[92] "Police 'Out to Kill' Suspected Burglar," *The Times*, November 23, 1996.

[93] Sue Clough, "Black Burglary Suspect's Death 'Was an Accident'," *The Daily Telegraph*, December 7, 1996.

Susan Price, who looked out her window at the events after hearing someone yell "black bastard," testified that she saw Mr. Douglas in the park lighted by the police flashlights. "His right hand was holding something up in the air," she said, "it was wooden but I couldn't tell exactly what he was holding. I could hear the police shouting 'drop the weapon.'" She reported that she then saw Mr. Douglas move deeper into the park as up to fifteen police outside shouted that if he dropped the weapon he would not get hurt. "I could see the black man was shaking. He looked terrified... He was not showing or doing anything of an aggressive nature... He dropped the wooden object. As soon as he did other police officers stormed into the park... the black man stepped back a couple of paces. Before those officers were on to him, the two [other officers] already in the park reached him first. "[94] She testified that the police attacked Mr. Douglas, "like dogs getting hold of a cat... I could hear the thud of the blows... it seemed to go on for ages, he was screaming... the police officers were hitting him in a hammering type action." She said that the police handcuffed the "whimpering man," "trussed up like a chicken" and tossed him into the police van, "like a sack of potatoes."[95]

Donna Sharpe, who also lived near the park, testified that the first thing she heard that night was somebody shouting the words, "black bastard."[96]

Despite these witness accounts, the three pathologists who examined him all agreed that his death was not the result of being beaten, and said that the evidence from their examinations did not indicate that Mr. Douglas was beaten with the severity that witnesses claimed.

The family's lawyer, Louise Christian, said that she would seek a judicial review because the coroner misadvised the jury about the requirements for an unlawful killing verdict. "There are two types of unlawful killing," she told *The Times,* "gross criminal negligence in not getting Mr. Douglas medical treatment or asking if he was all right, and unlawful force, because he was put on his front

---

[94] "Inquest Told Police Pounded on Black Man 'Like Dogs on a Cat'," *The Guardian,* November 22, 1996.

[95] Sue Clough,"Police Acted 'Like Dogs Chasing Cat'", *The Daily Telegraph,* November 22, 1996.

[96]"Inquest Told Police Pounded on Black Man 'Like Dogs on a Cat'," *The Guaridan,* November 22, 1996.

unnecessarily. The coroner said the jury had to find both things took place when in fact the jury had to find only one."[97]

Alton Manning, thirty-three years old, died in Blakenhurst Prison while being restrained on December 8, 1995. A Home Office post-mortem report by Helen Whitwell said that the events surrounding Mr. Manning, "fall into the category of death resulting from respiratory impairment and restriction during restraint. In this case there is evidence that airway occlusion arose due to pressure to the neck. In addition, restriction of chest movement while on the ground with pressure applied to the back of the chest would occur."[98] He was found with injuries on his face, head, and body. He had been complaining of harassment and violence from police and prison authorities for four years before his death. A spokesman for U.K. Detention Services said, "a violent struggle took place, and Mr. Manning was restrained and moved from the house unit. He became unwell and lost consciousness."[99]

Dennis Stevens, twenty-nine years old, was under restraint in a body belt when he was found dead in solitary confinement on October 18, 1995. No inquest has yet taken place. The CPS has yet to determine whether any criminal charges are to be brought against any of the police officers involved, and no inquest will be held until this has been determined.[100]

Brian Douglas, thirty-three years old, and a friend were approached by two officers at 12:30 a.m. on the night of May 3, 1995, in Clapham, London. There are conflicting accounts of what happened next, but the result was that Mr. Douglas

---

[97]Stephen Farrell, "Suspect's Death in Police Custody Was Accidental," *The Times*, December 7, 1996.

[98]Owen Bowcott, "Jail Death Raises Neck Hold Fears," *The Guardian,* February 3, 1996.

[99] Press Release from Birmingham Racial Attacks Monitoring Unit, January 10, 1996; Owen Bowcott, "Jail Death Raises Neck Hold Fears," *The Guardian*, February 3, 1996; "Prisoner dies in jail search," *Mail on Sunday*, December 10, 1995; "Family Demands Independent Inquiry into Prisoner's Death," *Press Association Newsfile*, December 10, 1995; "Cell death: Prisoner Alton Manning died in a struggle with warders at a prison in Worcestershire," *Sunday Mail*, December 10, 1995; "Man dies at private prison," *Sunday Times*, December 10, 1995.

[100] Jason Groves, "UK: Jail Cell Suicide Prompts Probe Bid," *Western Morning News*, July 17, 1996; David George, UK: Prisoner is Found Hanging in Cell," *Western Morning News*, February 16, 1996; *Searchlight*, December 1995; Human Rights Watch/Helsinki interview with Raju Bhatt, London, October 21, 1996.

was hit on the head with a baton. He was taken to Vauxhall police station, where a doctor examined him and determined that he was fit for detention. His condition worsened, and he was taken to St. Thomas' hospital where he died at 3:20 a.m. The two officers claimed that they had been acting in self-defense because Mr. Douglas was armed with a CS gas canister and a knife. They claimed that one of the officers struck one blow to Mr. Douglas' upper arm, which slid over his shoulder and hit his neck. But three pathologists gave evidence that the blow had been struck to the back right-hand side of his head, and several witnesses confirmed this account. No action was taken after a Police Complaints Authority investigation, and no charges were brought against the officers by the Crown Prosecution Service. An inquest jury announced on August 9, 1996, that Mr. Douglas' death was the result of "misadventure," not "unlawful killing." Coroner Sir Montague Levine stressed after the verdict that police should have better training in the use of batons and identifying injured people in custody.[101]

Omasase Lumumba, was arrested on September 15, 1991, in Catford and accused of stealing a child's bicycle.[102] He is the nephew of the first prime minister of what is now Zaire who was assassinated in 1961. Other members of his family were imprisoned, tortured and killed in Zaire. Mr. Lumumba was detained after an immigration officer discovered that he had applied for asylum in the United Kingdom and had entered the country under a false passport. After four days in a police prison he was transferred to Pentonville Prison. He was never informed about why he was being detained or what his rights were or what would happen to his case.[103]

---

[101] Lawrence Donegan, "Family of Dead Prisoner Seek Officers Suspension," *The Guardian*, May 15, 1995; Duncan Campbell, "Family of Dead Prisoner Seek Officers Suspension," *The Guardian*, May 15; Duncan Campbell, "Baton Query After Death in Custody," *The Guardian*, May 10, 1995; Jason Bennetto "Inquiry call after arrested man dies," *The Independent*, May 10, 1995; Jojo Moyes, "Police cleared on arrest death," *The Independent*, August 10, 1996; Duncan Campbell and Owen Bowcott, "Baton Death Verdict 'Unjust' Police 'need better training'," *The Guardian*, August 9, 1996; Stephen Wright and Cyril Dixon, "Anger as jury backs police in baton death," *Daily Mail*, August 9, 1996.

[102] Despite the arrest there is no record of him being charged for this offense.

[103] Principle 13 of the United Nations Body of Principles for the Protection of All Persons under Any Form of Detention or Imprisonment (Body of Principles); Article 9(2) of the International Covenant on Civil and Political Rights (ICCPR); and Article 5(2) of the European Convention for the Protection of Human Rights and Fundamental Freedoms (European Convention).

After periods of depression and being unable to eat, he was escorted to the hospital on October 8, 1991. On the way, he stopped and refused to move further. Three to four officers forced him into a cell in the segregation unit of the prison. Six to eight officers entered the cell. They ordered him to lie on the floor and pinned his arms, legs and head down. The officers forcibly stripped him of his clothing although prison regulations state that "a prisoner may [be] deprived of normal clothes only if, in the light of the individual case, this is considered essential to prevent self-injury or injury to others."[104] Despite this, officers testified at the inquest that there was no special reason to strip him and that it was "normal procedure" in the segregation block. Mr. Kenneth Richardson, a principal officer at Pentonville, stated that it was normal procedure to strip prisoners brought under control and restraint procedures. Some of Mr. Lumumba's clothes were cut off with scissors. Mr. Lumumba began struggling, but the officers continued to pin his limbs and head to the floor.

Dr. Daye Wanigaratne was called to apply a tranquilizing injection. He testified at the inquest that when he arrived he saw five to seven officers still pinning Mr. Lumumba to the floor even though he was limp and unconscious. He stated, "one officer was holding his head, two officers were holding his left and right arms and two officers were holding his left and right legs, and I think there were two others officers by the side."[105] Upon examination the doctor confirmed that he was dead.

The pathologist, Vesna Djuovic, found that there was a "strong possibility" that Mr. Lumumba had suffered an acute cardiac arrest following a prolonged struggle against restraint.

Andrew Durance who was a prisoner in a cell opposite Mr. Lumumba testified that he saw the officers kick and jump on Mr. Lumumba. He told the jury that once the officers realized he could see, he was moved to another cell and "two officers came to my door and said 'Don't go round telling anyone what you saw.'"[106]

In July 1993, an inquest jury found that Omasase Lumumba was unlawfully killed as a result of "use of improper methods of excessive force in the

---

[104] Prison Standing Order 3E, paragraph 24(3), December 1990.

[105] "Doctor Found Strip Cell Prisoner Dead," *Press Association Newsfile,* February 9, 1993.

[106]Melanue McFadyean, "Death in Cell 22," *The Guardian,* July 28, 1993.

process of control and restraint" by the officers. Despite this verdict, no disciplinary charges have been brought against the prison staff responsible.[107]

Ibrahima Sey, twenty-nine years old, a Gambian asylum-seeker, died on March 16, 1996, after he was taken into custody by Forest Gate police officers and transported to Ilford Police Station in east London. Mr. Sey had been arrested at 4:57 a.m. by police responding to a call from his wife regarding their domestic dispute. A mutual friend, Paebou Ndimbalan, accompanied Mr. Sey to the police station. Mr. Sey was not handcuffed and according to the friend went peacefully. Once at the station the police separated the two men. Mr. Sey became agitated and insisted that his friend be allowed to go with him. The friend stated, "The police created a barrier between us and then grabbed Ibrahima bringing him to the ground... As I was being led away, the last sight I had of Ibrahima was of him lying on his stomach, with the police pulling his arm around his back as if to handcuff him."

According to the Police Complaints Authority, "After negotiation by officers, this incident was peacefully resolved with Mr. Sey walking quietly out of the house and voluntarily getting into a police van, accompanied by a friend. He was then taken to Ilford police station. After peacefully leaving the police van, Mr Sey was showing signs of disturbed behavior. When officers went to lead him into the police station he became extremely violent and was restrained, during which handcuffs and CS [pepper] spray were used. The appropriateness of the use of CS

---

[107] Alan Travis, "No Prosecution Over Prison Death," *The Guardian*, December 10, 1993; Grania Langdon-Down, "Asylum Seeker's Death: No Court Action Against Officers," *Press Association Newsfile*, December 9, 1993; Heather Mills, "Family of custody victim wages fight for justice," *The Independent*, August 12, 1993; Heather Mills, "Death of asylum-seeker may lead to charges," *The Independent*, August 5, 1993; Grania Langdon-Down, "Jail Death Prosecutions Urged After Inquest Verdict," *Press Association Newsfile*, August 4, 1993; Heather Mills, "Asylum-seeker's jail death was unlawful," *The Independent*, July 28, 1993; Anne Benson, "Asylum Seekers's Killing Unlawful," *The Guardian*, July 28, 1993; Melanie Mcfadyean, "Death in Cell 22," *The Guardian*, July 28, 1993; Paul Myers, "Judges Order Jail Inquest to be Resumed," *The Guardian*, May 7, 1993; Mike Taylor, "Coroner 'Usurped Inquest Jury's Function'," *Press Association Newsfile*, May 4, 1993; "Coroner 'Erred in Cell Death Ruling'," *The Guardian*, February 24, 1993; "Stress of Struggle 'May Have Caused Remand Prisoner's Death'," *Press Association Newsfile*, February 11, 1993; John Carvel, "UK: Inquiry into Death of Asylum Seeker Held in Prison," *The Guardian*, October 11, 1991.

spray, at that time will be the subject of comment in the report of the investigation."[108]

According to police accounts, Mr. Sey then became unwell and was taken to a hospital where he died at 6:23 a.m. Only selective details of the post-mortem carried out the same day were made public, which included the provisional finding that his death followed a period of exertion and that Mr. Sey was suffering from hypertensive heart disease. A separate pathologist for Mr. Sey's family reported that there was no evidence to say that Mr. Sey suffered from heart disease.

Police statements indicate that CS spray was used on Mr. Sey while he was handcuffed. Reports from *The Independent* also indicated that at least five officers were attempting to restrain Mr. Sey at the time.

Guidelines regarding the use of CS spray issued by the Association of Chief Police Officers say that the spray should be used "primarily for self-defense... to provide officers with a tactical advantage in a violent encounter" and "primarily for dealing with violent subjects who cannot otherwise be restrained."

There have been a number of concerns raised about CS spray. Some evidence from the police monitoring organization, Statewatch, shows that the spray can cause lung damage and death to individuals suffering from asthma or using drugs, or who are subjected to restraining techniques which restrict the breathing passage. According to a Himsworth-Committee report when high levels of CS spray are used, heart failure, hepatocellular damage and death have been reported.

The evidence suggests that the police officers violated the guidelines by using the CS spray even though Mr. Sey was already being restrained by many officers and that this may have contributed to Mr. Sey's death.[109]

Police Brutality

There are a shocking number of incidents of police brutality, some of which appear to be racially motivated. Domestic and international human rights groups, including Human Rights Watch/Helsinki, the United Nations Committee to End Racial Discrimination (CERD), and the United States Department of

---

[108]"UK: Police Complaints Authority - Ibrahima Sey," *Hermes - UK Government Press Releases*, April 24, 1996.

[109]Jason Bennetto, "CS gas squirted at handcuffed man," *The Independent*, April 24, 1996; Statement by Amnesty International, October 11, 1996; "UK: Police Complaints Authority Completes Supervision of Ibrahima Sey Investigation," *Hermes - UK Government Press Releases*, December 11, 1996.

State,[110] have all raised concern at the level of police brutality against ethnic minorities in the U.K.

The following cases are only a few of the numerous reports received by Human Rights Watch/Helsinki of severe mistreatment of non-whites by the police. A number of the testimonies given to Human Rights Watch/ Helsinki could not be reported here because there are ongoing investigations. In other cases cited, the events took place several years before information became publicly available.

The United Nations and members of the Afro-Caribbean community in the UK have expressed deep concern that ethnic minorities are disproportionately victimized by police. These accounts of police brutality against ethnic minorities that explicitly or implicitly appear to be racially motivated[111].

On June 2, 1995, in an effort to mediate a dispute between **Mrs. Patel.** and two officials, the police entered Mrs. Patel's house. The fifteen-year-old daughter of Mrs. Patel did not want the police to enter her room.

> They dragged me down the stairs, threw me outside in the yard, and handcuffed me. Three officers were stepping on my ankles and wrists and hitting them with their truncheons. One officer was punching me in the head while I was lying on the ground. They were laughing. Other police officers there told them to leave me alone, but they kept on doing it. They said, "We are going to take the anger out of you." I was yelling to let me go, they kept saying, "shut up, Paki shit, Paki shit." Like a chant. I was crying. Then they picked me up and put me in the van. They hit me more there and harder because no one could see.
>
> They took me to the police station and put me in a cell. They told the clerk that I called them "white shit." They said to me, "Don't call us white shit again or we will kill you."

---

[110] U.S. Department of State, "United Kingdom of Great Britain and Northern Ireland," *Human Rights Practices 1995* (Washington: Department of State Dispatch, March 1996), Vol. 7.

[111]Human Rights Watch/ Helsinki also heard a number of reports regarding police brutality against whites. Because this report focused on racial violence they have not been included here.

I was in the cell for four hours. Then two social workers got me out. As I was leaving one officer said, "That is what you deserve Paki shit."[112]

Darren, sixteen years old:
On May 5, 1995, I was talking with friends around the shopping area. There was a big group of us. Someone must have called the police to get us moved. When the police arrived we were talking with one officer. He was reasonable. It was peaceful. Then we saw a kid who was being taken into a van shouting. The other kids were yelling that he had done nothing. They started throwing stones. The riot police were called and about thirty officers arrived. They were whacking kids across the back with their truncheons. One officer pushed Karen[113] down. I told him that she was pregnant. He hit her with a baton. Then he cracked me in the jaw. I picked up a sign to throw at him, but my brother knocked it out of my hands so I would not get in trouble. Police were everywhere.

Karen and I went to her house. The police came there looking for me. They dragged me to the police car and cuffed me. Karen's father said, "there are no marks on him, if there are any marks on him later there will be trouble." They were pushing me towards the car and tripped me as I was bending my head down to get in. They grabbed my head and rammed it into the car, "Black bastards, you are all scum," said one officer.

When I was in the car, they slammed my head against the window and slapped my face. Two officers got in the back seat with me. They kept punching me in the face and ribs. One officer was poking me in the ribs with his truncheon.

Once we arrived at the station, they picked me up and used my head to ram in the door like a battering ram. They dropped me

---

[112] Human Rights Watch/Helsinki interview with victim, London, July 2, 1995.

[113] The name has been changed to protect the identity of the witness.

to the floor and hit me with their truncheon on my ankles and legs and back.

In the charging room they slapped me in the face and said, "you black bastard, people like you are scum, do you want to feel pain, Nigger." They were laughing.

I was kicked in the groin and whacked on the back. One officer gripped me by the throat so I couldn't breathe. He said, "I've seen a black man cry, crying like a baby."[114]

On November 26, 1994, at 4:00 a.m., two police officers stopped **Thomas X.**[115] from entering his house, saying they wanted to take him to the station for questioning about his driving. They did not say that he was under arrest. Thomas X. tried to enter his house, but was blocked by one officer and pulled down the stairs by the other. Two friends of Thomas X. attempted to pull him away from the police. Eventually, he was taken into custody. Other police officers arrived. One officer pointed to **Samuel Y.**, saying that he would be taken in for obstruction. Several officers dragged him off, threw him on the ground. Witnesses stated that six to seven officers kicked and stamped on Samuel Y., mainly on his legs and ribs. The police also reportedly used their truncheons to hit him all over his body, although Samuel Y reported that he did not struggle or resist.[116]

In November 1994, the Metropolitan Police Commissioner agreed to pay £70,000 to **Mr. King**, thirty years old, in satisfaction of his claims pf assault and battery, false imprisonment and malicious persecution. The inquiry included accusations of assault, fabrication of evidence and false imprisonment by the two police officers and suggestions of a cover up in the investigation. In January 1991, Mr. King was driving his mini-cab when he was approached by two plainclothes officers who had emerged from an unmarked car. He said they grabbed him from behind by his neck and pulled him backwards onto the pavement. One officer held Mr. King by the neck in an armlock while leaning on his torso. Mr. King protested, asking if they were trying to kill him. One officer responded, "I'll kill you, you bastard" and punched him in the eye. The officers were joined by uniformed

---

[114] Human Rights Watch/Helsinki interview with victim, Neath, June 12, 1995.

[115] The name has been changed to protect the identity of the victim.

[116] Documents and testimonies submitted to Human Rights Watch/Helsinki, January 15, 1996.

officers. They took him to the police station where a doctor determined that the injury to his eye made him unfit to be detained in police custody and that he must be taken to the hospital. Mr. King was charged by the officers with possession of crack cocaine. He was acquitted of these charges.

At the time of the attack on Mr. King, the two officers were under investigation along with forty-five other officers at the Stoke Newington Police Station for misconduct. Mr. King's case was never considered in this inquiry although his allegations were consistent with a long list of misconduct for which the officers were being investigated.[117]

The police stopped **Hussein** for driving while disqualified in October 1994. Despite the low level of the offense they kept him in the cell from Saturday to Monday. While in the cell he rang a bell to request that he be allowed to use the toilet. The officers would not answer. He kept ringing. The police told him to shut up. He described what happened then:

> I called again. After twenty minutes one officer came and said, "What do you want." I said, "I want to go to the toilet" He said, "hold on," and walked away. He did not come back. I yelled at him to let me out. "Piss in the cell, spook. You can fucking wait, coon," he said.

> When they finally let me out, they were laughing. I went to the sergeant and asked why they would not let me out. "Piss off out of my face, who do you think you are, I got your food." I said, "what did I do to you."

> He grabbed me. I held on to his shirt, and asked again, "why didn't you let me out?" Two officers grabbed me from behind and pushed me over a desk and then back again. I lost my balance. I was still holding on to the sergeant's shirt. He started punching me in the chest.

> An officer grabbed my legs, and lifted me off the ground. "Let's give it to the black bastard," one said. They kept punching me in the chest.

---

[117] Press release from B.M. Birnberg & Co., solicitors for King, November 7, 1994; Human Rights Watch/Helsinki interview with solicitor, London, October 21, 1996.

> Then I heard a clunk. They had whacked me on the head and
> then hit my neck. After a few blows I was down on the floor. I
> tried to get up. One of the officers jumped up and landed with
> his heel on my chest.

> The sergeant got on top of me and punched me. He jabbed the
> front end of the truncheon in my ear. They dragged me into the
> cell and threw my body against the grill under the bed. They
> kept yelling stuff like "black bastard." They bashed me under the
> bed.[118]

On August 2, 1994, two police officers wanted to question **Mohammed G.** and bring him to the police station in connection with a burglary. His mother tried to grab him and pull him away from the officers. A police-community liaison, **Nasser**, calmly approached in an effort to quiet the situation.

Women and children gathered around and yelled at the police to let Mohammed go. Initially, to justify their behavior the police claimed that the crowd began throwing bricks, although later this account was retracted. Police also admitted that despite earlier claims to the contrary, Mohammed had not been seen by witnesses running on to the estate, nor that anybody in particular had been chased onto the estate.

One witness told the police they were upsetting the community. The police reportedly responded, "fuck the community, I don't want to talk about the community, just look at them." Eventually thirteen police vans or cars arrived. According to witness statements, the police came out swinging batons. Mohammed was grabbed and told he was being taken.

Nasser again tried to calm the situation. One officer approached him aggressively. Nasser passed the child he was holding to a woman standing behind him. The officer grabbed his right arm. Two or three other officers ran towards Nasser. They grabbed at his other arm and his legs and together with the original officer who had hold of Nasser's right arm, pulled him roughly away from the ramp. One witness stated, "The police simply rushed him away to a nearby car and threw him against it. He wasn't lashing out at the police, or trying to attack them in any kind of way." The officers held Nasser's arms and legs so that he was spread eagle on the car and hit his head on the windscreen.

---

[118] Human Rights Watch/Helsinki interview with victim and victim's solicitor, Cardiff, June 12, 1995.

A witness reported, "One officer got his baton out. I saw this go down towards the top half of Nasser's body." Nasser stated that "One officer called me a "cunt." "I was pinned down on the car, with a police officer on each arm. I was not struggling, as this was just not possible. Suddenly, I felt a huge blow on my face. I was clearly aware that this had come from one of the police officers around me, although at the time I did not know exactly how it had happened."[119]

In July 1994, **Martin K.**[120] was returning home when he noticed a police car and a group of officers on the road in front of his house. According to Martin K.'s report, the officers were standing by a car talking on the road in front of his house. When he looked to see what was going on, one of the officers shouted, "what are you looking at!" Martin K. responded, "what are you looking at?" The officer responded, "don't get cheeky, I'll nick you." Walking away, Martin K. replied, "I ain't done nothing." The officer shouted again, "don't walk away from me." He grabbed Martin K., pushed him on the ground and pressed his knee into his neck and upper back pinning him on the ground. Several other officers began punching and kicking Martin K. One officer held Martin K.'s neck and was choking him.

Martin K.'s mother came out of the house to see what the commotion was. When she saw the officers on top of her son, she pleaded with them to let her son go and tried to pull him away. Another officer came from behind her, twisted her arm behind her back and dragged her away. She was dragged to the police station barefoot. She asked the police officers to go slower because she was having trouble breathing and had recently been released from the hospital, but they ignored her.

Martin K.'s father then came out of the house to see twenty-five to thirty police officers and eight to ten police vehicles, his son pressed on the ground, and his wife being dragged away. "What is going on?" he shouted. Four to five officers ran towards the father. One of them head butted him. He was handcuffed and thrown to the ground. They picked him up and threw him down again four times, as Martin K.'s father kept asking, "what did I do?" The police officers took him to a police car.

Eventually, Martin K. was pulled to his feet and thrown into the back of a police van. One officer held him down and hit him several times, saying "I got

---

[119] Ibid.

[120] The name has been changed to protect the identity of the victim.

you now you little Paki." They took him to the police station. Once they arrived they dragged him out of the van by his legs.[121]

Daniel M.[122]:
Around March 1994, the police followed me in a car down the road. When I parked outside my sister-in-law's house, they parked in the middle of the road. One officer got out of the car and asked me where I was going, and he wanted to breathalyse me. I said, you want to do that in the middle of the street and kept walking. He walked away.

Then suddenly, I felt a sharp lash on the top of my head as I approached the house. They beat me down onto the pavement. "I've done nothing," I yelled. There were two officers. One of them pulled me back away from the building, the other one called for back-up. They kept hitting me and lashing me in the face. I was told later that there were ten police officers altogether.

I ran into the home of my sister-in-law to escape. The police followed me into the house. They kept beating me all over. They were yelling, "Break his fucking head, kill the black bastard." They knocked me unconscious. I guess they must have dragged me to a police van. I came to there, and they lashed me between my legs and then knocked me unconscious again. They said I stabbed a police officer. [He was later acquitted of the charge.] Now they stop me all the time. I don't like going out. I am a prisoner in my own home.[123]

On December 4, 1993, the police responded to a call indicating that there was a disturbance in a building in London. Police reported that they saw a boy crying, "leave me alone," at **David H.** They told Mr. H. to step away from the

---

[121] Documents and witness testimonies submitted to Human Rights Watch/Helsinki, July 21, 1995.

[122] The name has been changed to protect the identity of the victim.

[123] Human Rights Watch/Helsinki interview with victim and victim's sister-in-law, Liverpool, June 23, 1995.

child. They pulled Mr. H. away from the boy, but he tried to back towards the boy, ignoring them. The police arrested him for disorderly conduct. The mother of the child and friend of Mr. H. then entered the hallway and said that the police should let Mr. H. go. After some interchange between her and the police, she was arrested for disturbing the officers in the "lawful execution of their duty."[124]

David H. described what happened next:[125]

> On December 4, 1993, I went to help a friend with her child. As I was leaving, the police came from behind and told me to get away from the child. There was no problem, so there was no reason for them to say this. They handcuffed me. They hit me with a truncheon in the head. They said nothing. They took me down flights of stairs into a lift. They beat me onto the floor until I was unconscious. They threw me into the police van. When I came to, they said, "What are you doing here, you monkey nigger?" They started choking me, I turned to open the passage in my throat and passed out. At the police station, they wanted me to sign something. I refused. They beat me again in the cell. Later one officer came in and said, "you need medical help." I said, "I know." "You don't deserve it," he said.
>
> Now I suffer from constant head pain, nerve damage in my left hand, short-term memory loss, sweats and freezing. The police harass me now all the time. They follow me in their car, call me names. I started getting friends with me when I left the house. The police kept telling me to leave the area.
>
> Once I went to dump the trash. Two officers approached me and said, "Get out, you are taking up space, you should leave your house, we're going to get you in a few weeks."[126]

---

[124] Collated from documents submitted to Human Rights Watch/Helsinki, July 1995.

[125] The name has been changed to protect the identity of the victim.

[126] Human Rights Watch/Helsinki interview with victim and member of Newham Monitoring Project, London, July 10, 1996.

In June 1992, two officers visited the home of **Mrs. Imbert** in search of her son Jason, who they wrongly claimed was wanted. They found Colin at home and attempted to arrest him, saying that he was Jason. PC Plunkett refused to believe that Colin was not the man he was looking for. After challenging Colin, PC Plunkett repeatedly punched him, knocked him to the floor, and then radioed for back-up. When Mrs. Imbert tried to intervene, Plunkett struck her. As a result, she had to remain in the hospital for five days. Colin was charged with threatening behavior and assaulting an officer. Mrs. Imbert and Colin were awarded £28,000[127] and legal costs in a settlement against the police for assault and battery, wrongful detention, and malicious prosecution. Since the incident the police have been harassing Colin almost daily.[128]

In May 1992, PC Ryss Trigg was dismissed by a disciplinary tribunal of the PCA for having attacked and racially abused **Danny Goswell**, twenty-five years old, on November 12, 1990. Mr. Goswell and some friends were approached by Mr. Trigg and other officers and questioned about the car they were in. Mr. Goswell admitted to shouting at the officers. He was handcuffed and taken to the police station. At some point during the arrest Mr. Goswell was hit on the head with a truncheon by PC Trigg. Mr. Goswell asserted that he was beaten after the handcuffs were already placed on him. Mr. Goswell was initially convicted of assault and threatening behavior, but it was overturned later. Mr. Goswell suffered a number of injuries and required five stitches in his head. *The Observer* reported that the legal papers for the PC Trigg defense accepted blame, "the striking of the plaintiff by the said Trigg with the truncheon constituted the use of excessive force in all the circumstances and thus was an assault." In March 1993, Sir Paul Condon confirmed the dismissal of PC Trigg, after Mr. Trigg appealed to the commissioner. One month later Mr. Trigg appealed to the Home Office and a panel, chaired by James Anderton, the former chief constable of Greater Manchester, reinstated him.

On April 27, 1996, Mr. Goswell was awarded 120,000 pounds in compensation for assault, 12,000 pounds for false imprisonment following unlawful arrest and 170,000 pounds in punitive damages.[129]

---

[127] As of August 9, 1996, the British pound was worth 1.5490 per U.S. dollar.

[128] Duncan Campbell, "Police Ordered to Pay Family Pounds 28,000 for Attack by PCS," *The Guardian*, June 7, 1995; Human Rights Watch/Helsinki interview with Mrs. Imbert and member of Newham Monitoring Project, London, June 9, 1996.

[129] Duncan Campbell and Satish Sekar, "Policeman Told to Resign After Complaints of Racial Abuse," *The Guardian*, May 14, 1992; David Rose And Ken Hyder, "Sacked PC Given New Job by Met," *The Observer*, November 27, 1994; "Man hit with

In September 1995, **Aemer Anwar**, twenty-seven years old, was awarded £4,200 in compensation for having been attacked by PC Graham McKee and by Sheriff George Evans at Glasgow Sheriff's Court. According to news reports, on November 6, 1991, PC McKee found Mr. Anwar putting up posters. The officer chased Mr. Anwar up a grassy slope, knocked him down, banged his face against a concrete path, smashed Mr. Anwar's teeth and kicked him repeatedly on the ground. The officer exclaimed, "This is what happens to black boys with big mouths."

A statement by Sheriff Evans explained, "PC McKee then deliberately assaulted (him) by pulling back [Mr. Anwar's] head and slamming the bottom half of his face straight down onto the ground...PC McKee repeated the same action of pulling back the pursuer's head and pushing it down harder to the ground, causing the pursuer's mouth to hit the ground yet again. [Mr. Anwar] had the sensation of his teeth being crushed and at that point briefly lost consciousness."

Mr. Anwar was taken to Glasgow's Western Infirmary for treatment. He suffered bruising to his body and broken teeth. After the incident he suffered from post-traumatic stress and was unable to eat solids or live alone for several weeks.

Referring to police witnesses, the sheriff said, "All of their answers were just too pat and with a false ring of injured surprise. My overall impression (was) that the pursuer [plaintiff] and his witnesses had given an account that rang true, whereas the defender's witnesses [the police] had presented a suppressed version of events in a concerted effort to sanitize the actions that night of PC McKee." He added that the attack appeared to be racially motivated.

A witness told the court that he saw the officer kicking Mr. Anwar, while another policewoman was also nearby. He also said, "My impression was the police officer was taunting him, almost leering at him... it was quite horrific to see the policeman kick someone on the ground. Police are there to protect you."

Mr. Anwar was provided assistance from the Scottish Council for Civil Liberties. After receiving the compensation, Mr. Anwar said, "It raises the question of how many other people in this position have not had the level of support I had and were forced to walk away."

Despite the findings of Sheriff Evans, PC McKee only faced a six-week suspension for his racially charged assault. In a public statement, Superintendent Louis Munn of Strathclyde Police said, "The prosecutor has since intimated that

---

truncheon is awarded pounds 300,000," *The Daily Telegraph*, April 27, 1996; Human Rights Watch/Helsinki interview with Dev Berrah of GACARA, London, June 30, 1995.

he is to take no proceedings. The thirty-five-year-old officer concerned has since been returned to duty and the matter rests with the deputy chief constable."[130]

On June 20, 1995 **Edmund Lawrence**, thirty-two years old, was paid £26,000 in damages after he charged that he was assaulted, racially abused, and wrongfully arrested. In December 1989, he was arrested near his home in New Cross on suspicion of having a defective car headlamp. During the arrest, he said, the police grabbed his arms and tried to drag him to the ground while one officer said, "Get the black cunt on the floor." The other officers punched him in the stomach and kicked him in the head.

After being taken to the police station to be fingerprinted, Mr. Lawrence said that his hands were hurt. The officers forced him to the ground, while one said, "Hold him down, I am going to show him what pain is." The officer pressed a truncheon into Mr. Lawrence's ankle saying, "Are you going to let us take your prints now?" The police charged him with assaulting a police officer, but he was acquitted at Camberwell Green magistrates in July 1990.[131]

On May 6, 1991, **Clare**, **Ken**, and **Terry** went to the police station because they were told **Paul** had been taken there under suspicion of being involved in a crime. Terry is the father of Clare, 30, Ken, 13, and Paul, 15. Ken, after repeatedly inquiring about the whereabouts of Paul and receiving hostile responses, three officers jumped over the counter to grab them:

---

[130] Graeme Stewart, "Police face prosecution threat," *The Scotsman*, November 10, 1995. See also, "Cop Faces Race Rap," *Daily Record*, November 10, 1995; *Press Association Newsfile*, November 9, 1995; Severin Carrell, "Police leader objects to constable's suspension," *The Scotsman*, September 23, 1995; "Support for Race Case PC," *Daily Record*, September 23, 1995; Severin Carrell, "Policeman suspended after student wins race attack case," *The Scotsman*, September 22, 1995; Severin Carrell, "The thin blue veneer, Scottish Police Forces Have Anti-Racist Strategies, Yet The Equality Plans Drawn Up At Headquarters Cannot Be Guaranteed To Reach The Streets," *The Scotsman*, September 22, 1995; "Policeman in race attack suspended," *The Daily Telegraph*, September 22, 1995; Lachie Kennedy, "PC suspended as 'racist victim' awarded 4,200 pounds," *The Herald (Glasgow)*, September 22, 1995; "Policeman suspended after race bias ruling," *The Independent*, September 22, 1995; Erlend Clouston, "Race Attack Policeman Suspended," The Guardian, September 22, 1995; John Clark, "Police Officer Suspended After Race Attack Ruling," *Press Association Newsfile*, September 21, 1995; "Policeman denies assaulting student," *The Herald (Glasgow)*, April 29, 1995.

[131] Duncan Campbell , "UK: Assault Costs Met Pounds 26,000," *The Guardian*, June 21, 1995.

Clare: One of the officers got behind me and put me in a head lock. Two others grabbed my arms. Ken said, "What are you arresting my sister for?" The inspector then said [pointing to Ken] "Nick that one too." Three police officers grabbed him. One of them kneed him in the belly. They were shouting at us, "You dirty black bastards!" They took Ken into a cell and drew down the shutter over the door. They took me into a changing room. I said, "What are you doing with my brother, he's only thirteen!"

I heard Terry shout from another room, "What are you going to do, kill me?" He shouted like he was in pain. I told an officer who was with me, "That's my dad, he is just an old man, he can't take a beating."[132]

Terry: I said what is all this for? The inspector said, "Nick that man too." I felt a group of men lift me off the ground from behind. They put me on the floor in a room and removed my shoes. They were pulling my feet back and forth so that it was agony. They pulled my arms up behind my back. I was screaming in pain, "You're going to kill me, you are going to give me a heart attack." One of the officers stamped on my forehead and said, "Shut up you dirty nigger." He talked with the other officers while this was going on. Then he said, "Take his trousers off." They undid my fly, turned me over onto my belly and took off my trousers. One of the officers put his knee into the right side of my chest. Another officer put his knee into the left side and they both held my hands behind my back. They kept twisting my hands. Then someone said, "Jump on him." One of the officers got up off my back and jumped on me. He said, "Search his pockets to see if there is anything to kill the black bastard." They searched my pocket and laughed. I felt my breath leave my body. My hands went numb. Then they got off my back, turned me over, carried me, and threw me onto the floor in a cell. I could not get up. I was in agony. Later the cell window opened. I heard someone yell my name, and then tell me they were not going to charge me.

---

[132] Human Rights Watch/Helsinki interview with Clare, London, July 15, 1995.

I have been in physiotherapy many times since. My faith in the police is shattered. I do not go out anymore and can't work.[133]

Failure to Respond Effectively to Racially Motivated Violence

Human Rights Watch/Helsinki recognizes the unequivocal condemnation by Chief Police Constable Sir Paul Condon of racist violence and his emphasis on the important role the police must play to stop it. In his first major speech to a conference on racial and sexual harassment, he stated that "the police must be intolerant of those who indulge in racially motivated abuse, and intolerant of those who use hatred and violence as the tools of their own expression. But if we are to be intolerant of those outside the police service who fail to treat their fellow human beings with dignity and respect, we must be equally intolerant of our own colleagues who fail to reach the required standards."[134]

There are numerous local initiatives to improve police response to racially motivated violence. While Human Rights Watch/Helsinki welcomes these efforts, they are often too few, and often have uncertain effects.

Community leaders and victim support groups frequently testified that such initiatives were "mere public relations gimmicks" with little practical effect on the ground. Others interviewed by Human Rights Watch/Helsinki indicated that despite the well intentioned and appreciated institutional structures that have been developed from the higher ranks of the police force, many lower ranking officers do not live up to acceptable standards of policing. Moreover, there is insufficient evidence that the police are willing to clamp down on incidents of racist violence and racist behavior by their own officers and to hold their officers accountable for violating the principles articulated by Police Commissioner Condon.

Although many of those interviewed by Human Rights Watch/Helsinki were victims of racist violence and harassment over a period of years, they often stopped reporting incidents to the police because the authorities seemed unable or unwilling to investigate the crimes effectively. Confidence that the police will fairly and effectively respond to racist violence is very low. Typical statements by victims and community groups include: "The police just don't care," "They never do anything," "They don't take racist violence seriously," "They come look around as if they are bored and then leave," "Sometimes they threaten you for having called them for help."

---

[133] The case was also discussed with Terry, London, July 15, 1995, and their solicitor, July 3, 1995.

[134] Police Review, March 5, 1993.

According to a study covering the area of Newham, 54 percent of the victims of racially motivated incidents were dissatisfied with the police response, and only 27 percent were satisfied.

It is very difficult to determine in which cases and to what degree poor responses by the police are due to racism, a lack of resources, the lack of professionalism of senior officers, the inexperience of junior officers, and/or a lack of effort. In a number of testimonies given to Human Rights Watch/Helsinki it was clear that some cases were very difficult to investigate effectively even by the best officers with the best intentions. The resources do not exist to probe thoroughly every incident of low level racist harassment. There are also legitimate legal factors intended to protect citizens' rights and privacy that can constrain police investigations. However, even taking these factors into consideration, they do not provide an adequate explanation for the numerous accounts of lax or hostile policing reported in the U.K.

Human Rights Watch/Helsinki heard testimony from victims, solicitors and community groups that indicated that all of these factors are part of the picture. Many added, however, that in cases where lack of effort and racism played a role there were few effective means of holding those officers accountable for their behavior.[135]

Clear-up rates for racially motivated incidents have varied widely over the years, but are lower than many other crimes. In 1987, 30 percent of the racially motivated cases reported were cleared up, in 1990 the figure was only 13 percent, while in 1993 the rate rose to 22 percent.[136] This compares to a roughly 75 percent clear-up rate for "Wounding" offenses, 75 percent for "Threat, etc. to Commit Criminal Damage," 51 percent for "Criminal Damage Endangering Life," and 26 percent for all noticeable offenses in 1993.[137] According to Sajide Malik of the

---

[135] It is police policy not to discuss specific cases, making it impossible to track the outcome of misconduct complaints against the police. It is important to note that the police cannot be sued for negligence of duty. This leaves complainants at the disposal of internal investigations, or in very serious complaints, the Police Complaints Authority (PCA), or in limited cases to file civil actions.

[136] Home Affairs Committee, *3rd Report*, p. xiii.

[137] Home Office *1993 Criminal Statistics England and Wales* (London: HMSO, 1993).

Newham Monitoring Project, "Police officers who have attacked or killed black people are still on duty. They may pay a fine, but they are still on the streets."[138]

In the past few years, the cases of Muktar Ahmed and Stephen Lawrence have been frequently cited as examples of the failure by police to respond to racist violence. Human Rights Watch/Helsinki heard testimony from several other victims whose cases were handled ineffectively or with hostility.

The attack on **Muktar Ahmed** (see chapter on Racially Motivated Violence) was widely publicized. Since the incident, a number of serious concerns have surfaced about whether the police properly investigated the crime.

According to Joy Meriam, the defense lawyer for one of Mr. Ahmed's attackers, the police stopped investigating after they secured enough evidence to prosecute her client. There were written diaries submitted by a friend of the attackers that implicated several others, and singled out one individual as the ring leader, but this was not seriously investigated. Additionally, the friends of Muktar's who escaped being attacked themselves told the police they could identify some of the gang, but they were not called for an identification parade.[139]

In response to tremendous media attention, the police stressed that they were taking the incident seriously and had undertaken an unusually extensive investigation. Despite these claims, however, the fact that the other members of the gang were not charged or more effectively investigated is troubling. Police give the impression that the alleged perpetrators of such crimes can escape serious investigation or punishment, reinforcing the community's belief that the police do not take violence against them seriously.

F:
In March 1995, I opened the door to see what set off the car alarm. As soon as I opened the door I was picked up by my upstairs neighbors [who were standing outside], dragged along the passageway. One of them asked me how long till my baby was expected. I told them not long. They punched me in the stomach. I kicked back. One woman hit me in the face. They dragged me to the staircase leading upstairs. There I saw five other women. One man grabbed me by the hair and lifted me up.

---

[138] Human Rights Watch/Helsinki interview with caseworker Sajide Malik from Newham Monitoring Project, London, June 15, 1995. This sentiment was widespread.

[139] Human Rights Watch/Helsinki interview with Joy Meriam, April 10, 1995, and Vicram Dodd, April 5, 1995; documents submitted to Human Rights Watch/Helsinki.

They kicked and punched me in the stomach, saying, "I hope you lose your baby." They kicked me between my legs. I got away and called the police. The police came and were sympathetic. They took me to the hospital. But after that they never seemed to question anyone. They did not speak to any of the neighbors to see if they saw anything.[140]

During the month of May 1994, Asian youth were repeatedly attacked and harassed but the police took little action either to protect the victims or to identify the perpetrators. The following cases are typical of numerous reports received by Human Rights Watch/Helsinki.

Ishmail K. and Mustak K.:

Six to seven white lads from the Manor Estate came on Staniforth Road. They came in two cars. They beat up three kids. They were yelling things like, "black bastards get out." They smashed up a car and left. The police came but did not seem interested and did not look for witnesses. We gave the police registration numbers for the cars.

A few days later, adults came with bats and sticks to beat people up again. We picked up stones to defend ourselves. They [the white men] left. They returned at night for a bigger fight.

Every day these white gangs would come in their cars to beat us up. The police would come, but they never did anything. Every time we made complaints, they would say, "you are wasting our time, there is no one here. If you call again we will arrest you." Every night police would be called, and the whites would run. These attacks escalated, and we started to hit back.

Gangs of white men in their twenties with sticks and clubs would come to attack Asian lads who were only fourteen or fifteen. One white man smashed a car windscreen of an Asian lad. The police arrived in riot vans and cars and told everyone to clear off. When the Asian lad did not move immediately he was arrested and was kept in a cell overnight. Another young Asian

---

[140] Human Rights Watch/Helsinki interview with victim, London, July 10, 1995.

boy was arrested for fingering an officer. Some kids began throwing small rocks. The police then started arresting kids at random. In all, eight Asian boys were arrested. They were brutal. One officer sat on Ishmail. To Mustak one officer said, "you black bastards, you run like mad when you see the police." None of the white men were arrested even though the men who smashed the windscreen were standing there, and we told the police who it was.[141]

In 1994, in Sheffield, a white family repeatedly banged on the door of a **Somali family** and yelled, "We want you out of here, we are going to kill you." One member of the family reported:

I could not understand everything. They yelled such terrible things. We did not answer because we were afraid. I took the children upstairs. They smashed the window in. There were two adults and five children. One woman had a knife. The other one had an iron bar. Many people joined in from all over. A police car came from over the hill. They must have seen the crowd standing outside yelling. When it got closer the people dispersed into their houses. The officers did not question anyone.

One officer stayed with us. Later, one woman and six children returned. They left when they saw the officer was still with us. The police did not question anyone. They know that this is a racist area. We told the police that this was the woman who broke the window. They did nothing. The police told us to just forget about it.

At one point the police installed a hotline so they should come after five minutes. But they always come too late and look around casually and then leave.

In July 1994, at 3:00 p.m. a man and a woman with a dog and two kids smashed our door. The man was holding a knife. We

---

[141] Human Rights Watch/Helsinki interview with victim, Sheffield, June 28, 1995. Three other victims and their solicitor were also interviewed by Human Rights Watch/Helsinki.

ran upstairs into the bathroom. They came in and smashed our
room. When they left we came out and pressed the panic button.
The police came after half an hour. They saw the smashed door.
The two attackers were outside. They were shouting. The police
did not question them. They told us to stay inside. "If I see you
outside, you will be arrested for anything that happens."[142]

The area has figured prominently in the news as having a serious problem
with racist violence. In 1993, ten Somali refugees were driven out of their homes
due to ongoing harassment and violence. During the previous two years the twelve-
year-old son of one of the families had been abducted and beaten unconscious,
other children and women had been beaten, and windows had been regularly
smashed.[143]

Sunil I. was attacked on November 17, 1994, as he was coming out of
school:

When I saw the three boys waiting for me, I tried to run back
into the canteen. They rushed me. They had a knife and a
baseball bat. They were punching me and kicking me. They used
their knife, and I had to get stitches in my head. They kept
hitting my body with the bat. They knocked me unconscious....
I did not return to school for a month because I was afraid.

The two admitted to the attack. Many people were there when it
happened so there were many witnesses. I wanted to go to court.
It was not until January 24, 1995, that I finally received a police
letter that they were cautioned for actual bodily harm. They only
sent this letter after pressure from my solicitor. It is not enough.
They beat me unconscious. They should get more than a
caution.[144]

In September 1993, **Kapil**, fifteen years old, was coming home from
school when he was chased by a white man about thirty years old. The man chased

---

[142]Human Rights Watch/ Helsinki interview with victim, Sheffield, June 28, 1995.

[143]David Rose, "UK: Refugees Flee Estate Racism," *The Observer*, August 15,
1993; Human Rights Watch/Helsinki interview with victims, Sheffield, June 28, 1995.

[144] Human Rights Watch/Helsinki interview with victim, London, July 1, 1995.

Kapil all the way home, and Kapil was just able to shut the door behind him. The man began banging on the door yelling, "I'm going to cut you, Paki shit. Come out!" The boy's twelve-year-old sister called the police. By the time the police arrived the man had left and after hearing the description of what happened from the girl, said, "What are you telling us? A children's story. If you want to call us again make up a better story." The police did not question Kapil about the incident. Two months earlier Kapil had been attacked in the street by another white man. He was beaten to the ground and hospitalized overnight.

The family is regularly harassed and sometimes attacked by neighbors. As Kapil reported:

> Twice a week they would bang on our doors, saying stuff like, "Pakis get out!" They urinate on our doorstep. They throw wine bottles at the door. On June 10, 1995, our neighbor was banging on our door again shouting for us to get out. I called the police. He stopped when they came. When they left, the man started again. I called the police again. The second time the police told me that if I called them again they will arrest me. I asked them what I should do. I do not want to be attacked again. They said, just buggar off. They left us in a helpless situation.

> Incidents like these have been going on since we moved in 1989. Back then my father was attacked so badly that his arm was broken, and they had to put a metal plate in his arm. I was also attacked twice. Once in 1989 and once in 1990.[145]

Farouk H. was punched in the face and head, and racial insults were shouted at him by two white men. The police arrived, and he described the incident. While he was talking with the police, he saw the two men emerge from a post office in the same street and identified them to the police. The police spoke to the men and searched them. The men reportedly confessed to attacking Farouk but were neither arrested nor detained. One of the officers told Farouk that they would visit him over the weekend to follow up on the case, but they did not take his name or address and received no documentation of the incident. When the

---

[145] Human Rights Watch/Helsinki interview with Kapil, London, July 15, 1995, and written testimony dated June 25, 1995.

station was called and asked what was happening, there was no record of the incident.[146]

On Thursday, May 11, 1995, after getting punched and beaten by a white man, **Wahid** went to the police station to report the case and give the plate number for the car of his attacker. There were many people who saw the incident. His eye was bleeding badly and his knee was bruised.

> I went to the police station straight-away but the officer on duty was busy inquiring whether the person in front of me could put spiked wire on his fence or not. After twenty minutes she very casually took my report. She was taking it very lightly and did not even bother to take photographs or look at my injuries. No action appeared to have been taken since then.[147]

Mohammed W., a fifty-five-year-old Somali man, reported to Human Rights Watch/Helsinki that:

> In the summer of 1992 around 7:00 p.m. I was visiting a friend about her problems with skinheads in the area. They were harassing her and had beaten her. As I was approaching her flat, I saw a group of men standing around. One of the men whistled and nine or ten men came at me from different directions. They beat me with baseball bats until I was unconscious. My friend called the police, but they did not come. I went to the hospital. I had to get myself there on my own, even though I had blood pouring down my face. While I was there some of the guys who attacked me arrived. One of them said he had a broken thumb. I told the nurse that these were the guys who attacked me. One of the men said, "You are still alive. We came to finish you." They launched at me. I jumped behind a table to protect myself. The police were called. Three of them ran away before the police got there. The police went to question the ones who were left. They never questioned the people in the waiting room about

---

[146] Document submitted to Human Rights Watch/Helsinki by CAPA, July 21, 1995.

[147] Human Rights Watch/Helsinki interview with victim, London, June 13, 1995. The case was also discussed with Dev Berreh of GACARA, London, June 13, 1995.

what happened. They never questioned my friend who saw the incident from the beginning. I heard later that one of them eventually pleaded guilty to grievous bodily harm and got a suspended sentence. I was never called to court. There were no charges against any of the others. My friend was never called to an identification parade.

My friend faced harassment for months after that. They threw eggs and stones at her. She was hospitalized after one of the attacks. They put dog shit at her door. They said that if she called the police, they would burn the house. Eventually she just fled the flat. Now the council has moved someone else in the same place. They fled after they were threatened.[148]

John, a sixteen-year-old Asian boy, described his experiences with police protection:

On October 18, 1993, me and me mate were coming out of school. We saw thirty-five white guys, some older skinheads. They were waiting by the DLR station. They saw us coming out of school. Me and me mate went around the building, but they followed us. Me mate said, "let's run." I thought he was joking. I did not know what these white guys were going to do. I was innocent then. I thought they might be looking for someone, not me. I just stood there. They surrounded me. I could have run, but I did not think. One came up and punched me. Another kicked me to the ground. Then they all started kicking and punching me. I covered myself. I was looking for someone to help me. Then I saw a police van just passing by. They did not even stop.

White boys and Asian boys always fight. When Asian boys bring their back-ups the police are always there to protect the white boys, but if the white boys bring back-ups the police are never there and we get beaten. Now we never even bother to call the police. Me mate was beaten so bad, he was in the hospital for a whole day. There was seven to eight white boys, eighteen years old. They had knives. He never came back to school. He was too

---

[148] Human Rights Watch/Helsinki interview with victim, London, June 19, 1995.

afraid. He did not report the incident to anyone. He did not trust them.[149]

Sixteen-year-old **Mohammed**, from London, reported that:

As soon as we moved in here in 1989 the trouble started. People come banging on our door, shouting "Paki get out" and that lot. Back then my parents were walking from shopping, and someone stabbed my father and hit my mother on the shoulder. My father now has a metal plate in this arm. Later that year my brother was badly beaten up by seven or eight white blokes who jumped out of a car. The next summer I was attacked by five guys near a pub... The police never do anything. Then, again in 1993, my brother was attacked again so badly that he was in the hospital overnight. This time the police came, but instead of investigating they said, "What are you doing around here?" As if he did not belong here. They did not follow up. People saw what happened, but they were not questioned.

People are always throwing stones at him [the brother], and they spit on me. They put feces on the door, or urinate. They wrote on our walls, last year, "Blacks get out!" Once my neighbor was banging on the door yelling "Pakis, get out." I was afraid he would smash the window so I called the police. He did not do anything. I called again. He went to talk to my neighbor who told the officer that I had attacked him. The officer told me that if I called again about the neighbor I would be nicked for wasting his time. I have had enough of the police. I do not know what to do![150]

False Arrests/Arresting the Victim
Ethnic and racial minorities not only report the failure of the police adequately to investigate racially motivated crimes, they also report that they are

---

[149] Documents and testimonies submitted to Human Rights Watch Helsinki, July 19, 1995.

[150] Human Rights Watch/Helsinki interview with victim, London, July 21, 1995. The case was also discussed with Ranjit Lohia of CAPA, London, July 21, 1995.

often presumed to be the guilty party in any conflict with whites. According to the human rights group Liberty, "ethnic minorities are disproportionately subject to arbitrary arrests and detentions."[151] Shoddy investigations by police into incidents of racist violence can lead to the victim being arrested. In some cases Afro-Caribbean and Asian families who have been victimized for months or years by the same people attempt to protect themselves during another attack and are arrested themselves, while their attackers walk free. In these situations the police are often aware of the history, but seem to ignore it.

In other cases, officers become confused at the scene of an incident because emotions are high and various contradictory accusations are made. While this does pose a challenge, police are trained professionals. It is their duty to cope with complex situations properly, effectively, and without bias. The situation is further complicated by language barriers between white officers and some Asian victims. As a result, officers reportedly have a tendency to favor accounts given by the white attackers whom they understand better. It is very important in this context that interpreters be provided in order to improve the chances that accounts given by Asians at the scene of the incident will be properly considered.

For example, the restaurant of an Asian man, **Muktar P.**, was attacked regularly by gangs of youths yelling racist abuse, setting rubbish alight, firing at the staff with air guns, writing graffiti, throwing eggs and on one occasion a fire rocket was launched through the staff toilet window. The police were called repeatedly. Notes taken by Mr. P during these incidents say, "Police did not seem to do much about it..." These incidents continued until twenty to thirty youths attacked the restaurant. The owner was hit by a car and surrounded by twenty youths. He suffered injuries to his arm and shoulder. During the scuffle he tried to defend himself. When the police arrived Mr. P was charged with three counts of assault and possession of a dangerous weapon (a mop handle). None of his attackers were caught or charged.[152]

In April 1994, **Mr. Oussman** heard loud bangs on his front door. When he investigated the noise he saw ten to fifteen white youths throwing bricks and shouting racist abuse outside. In the past when he called the police, their efforts left him unsatisfied because they could not find sufficient evidence to arrest the perpetrators. As a result, he went after the assailants himself and disarmed one of

---

[151] Liberty Human Rights Convention, Report 3: The Destruction of Civil and Political Liberties (London: National Council for Civil Liberties, 1993), p. 25.

[152] Case submitted to Human Rights Watch/Helsinki from community group, Support Against Racist Incidents (SARI).

them. Six police officers eventually arrived and charged Mr. Oussman with affray and assault.

The attacks on his house by the same groups continued after this incident. They have smashed his windows, broken fanlights and painted graffiti. Though he has called the police on numerous occasions, they have made no concerted effort to investigate these incidents.[153]

On May 20, 1992, three plainclothes officers arrived at **Mr. Rehman's** home. When he answered the door one of the officers flashed a card and entered the house. When Mr. Rehman asked to see a warrant the officer said, "We don't need one pal." All three officers entered the house. They searched his bedroom, drawers and cupboards. They said they were searching for a pad on which Mr. Rehman had allegedly written a threatening letter. They did not say anything more about the letter.

On the way to the station the police said they were told that the letter was written "in typical nigger fashion," adding, "it's got to be you." After fingerprints were taken he was told that he would not be charged. He was not given a search record nor was he cautioned or informed of the reason for his arrest.

The Crown Prosecution Service (CPS) recognized that there was sufficient evidence to justify the institution of criminal proceedings against one of the officers for false imprisonment, but they chose not to on the grounds that it was not in the public interest.[154]

On July 27, 1993, **Mr. Ajakaiye** went to Shooters Hill police station to report that a stereo tape recorder/radio had been stolen from his fiancée's car. When he reported the theft to the officer at the desk the officer questioned him about his immigration status. When he told the officer that he was British, the officer told him that he was a liar and that he was under arrest. Mr. Ajakaiye left the station to try and speak with his fiancée outside. He was then surrounded by several officers, grabbed by the left wrist and handcuffed. He was told that he was under arrest for assaulting a police officer.

He was taken to the Plumstead police station where he was told that he had been arrested on suspicion of an immigration offense and for assault on a police officer. He was detained from 9:12 p.m. to 12:40 a.m. Between 10:00 and 11:10 at night he was taken in handcuffs to his home address by officers in order

---

[153] Human Rights Watch/Helsinki interview with Dev Berreh of GACARA, London, June 30, 1995; case history submitted to Human Rights Watch/Helsinki by Mr. Berreh.

[154] Official documents submitted to Human Right Watch/Helsinki, July 21, 1995.

to search for his passport. He showed the officers his passport and other documentation. The officers continued to search through his things even after he presented his documents. The officers took him back to the police station and detained him for another hour and a half even though they had confirmed he had a British passport.

Ajakaiye's case was settled by the police on March 17, 1995, for an undisclosed amount in damages for false imprisonment and assault. This settlement avoided a civil action suit against the police for racial discrimination.[155]

Treatment in Prisons

The Home Office has concluded that the level of racist violence and abuse in prisons is far higher than reported. The study interviewed 501 inmates in eight prisons: among them, 128 were white, 220 black, seventy-five Asians, and seventy-eight from other ethnic groups. Although the Prison Service only reported twenty-two incidents in prisons throughout England and Wales in 1991, more than half of the black inmates interviewed in the study said they had been victimized by staff on the basis of their race. One third of the Asian prisoners and one quarter of those from other ethnic groups had the same experience. Black prisoners interviewed said each had suffered an average of seven incidents during the previous three months.

The study also indicates that while a race relations policy was adopted by the Prison Service in 1983, three quarters of the officers have not read the manual. This is a clear failure of effective training of prison staff.[156] A number of prisons since the study have reportedly established race relations representatives to facilitate the reporting of racist incidents and complaints.[157]

Stop and Search

The PCA and others have expressed concern that ethnic minorities are stopped and searched disproportionately more often than whites. The PCA annual report for 1993/94 stated: "We are particularly concerned about the number of people of minority ethnic origin who are stopped and searched by the police. The

---

[155] Human Rights Watch/Helsinki interviews with Dev Berrah, London, June 30, 1995; Human Rights Watch/ Helsinki interview with Jane Deighton, London, July 3, 1995; documents submitted to Human Rights Watch/Helsinki.

[156] Alan Travis, "Hidden Face of Prison Racism," *The Guardian*, November 7, 1994.

[157] Human Rights Watch/Prison Project, *Prison Conditions in the United Kingdom* (New York: Human Rights Watch, 1992) p. 50.

figures for 1993-94 suggest that 25 percent were from minority ethnic communities that only represent some five percent of the total population."

Despite such official expressions of concern, the police have continued aggressive stop and search practices. Again, in 1995/96, the PCA reiterated its concern stating: "We continue to be concerned by mounting evidence that members of minority ethnic groups are being disproportionately subjected to police 'stop and search'. The fact that only a small proportion of these stops result in an arrest suggest that a number are merely random 'fishing trips' which do nothing to improve relations between the police and minority communities."[158]

The PCA found that in 1995/96 complaints resulting from stop and search powers accounted for 13 percent of all cases reported that year. Of these complaints regarding stop and searches, 29 percent were made by blacks. From the year before, these figures reflect a 2 percent drop in complaints regarding stop and searches, but 7 percent more from blacks[159]. This may reveal that not only are blacks filing disproportionately more complaints than whites, but that this imbalance in increasing. The report also showed that complaints regarding stop and searches from blacks accounted for 25 percent of all complaints from this group. Only 4 percent of complaints regarding stop and searches were made by Asians. Stop and search complaints made up 14 percent of all complaints by Asians.

Complaints about stop and search practices are particularly intense in London. The Metropolitan Police Service accounts for 51 percent of all stop and search cases, and 44 percent of all stop and search cases in the Metropolitan Area were made by black people. Thus, according to the PCA, 79 percent of all stop and search complaints filed by black people were against the Metropolitan Police.

---

[158] Police Complaints Authority, *Annual Report 1995 - 1996* (London:HMSO, 1996), p.47.

[159] Police Complaints Authority, *Annual Report 1995-1996*(London:HMSO, 1996).

STOP AND SEARCH
January-September 1994 Figures for Metropolitan Police[160]

Borough	Percentage of black people	Percentage of ethnic minority people in population
Brent	46.47	16.51
Haringey	44.99	17.09
Hackney	44.05	22.00
Lambeth	43.50	21.82
Wandsworth	39.38	10.62
Lewisham	38.58	16.25
Hammersmith & Fulham	36.57	10.19
Southwark	32.89	17.76
Waltham Forest	31.32	11.28
Kensington & Chelsea	28.80	5.84
Islington	28.68	10.59
Newham	27.11	14.36
Ealing	26.11	7.07
Camden	20.98	5.51
Croyden	20.69	7.57
Westminster	20.41	7.71
Harrow	16.62	3.72
Tower Hamlets	15.12	7.08
Greenwich	13.03	5.36
Merton	12.51	5.74
Hounslow	12.32	2.74
Barnet	11.98	3.57
Enfield	11.61	6.17
Redbridge	11.47	4.24
Richmond upon Thames	9.97	0.75
Barking & Dagenham	9.08	2.33
Bromley	7.65	1.56
Hilingdon	5.08	1.65
Sutton	4.68	1.38
Kingston upon Thames	3.66	0.97
Havering	3.25	0.95
Bexley	1.06	1.40
Total	25.93	

These figures show two trends. First, in some areas Afro-Caribbeans can represent almost 50 percent of all stop and searches. Second, blacks are often over-

---

[160] A police officer can legally stop and search a person if the officer has reasonable grounds for suspecting that the person has: stolen property, an offensive weapon, an article for use in burglary or theft, or firearms.

represented most in those areas where there is a proportionally small black population. Most importantly these figures suggest that police think of blacks as more likely to be criminals and thus search them more often.

Similar patterns are found in Greater Manchester. Twenty-seven ethnic minority members for every one thousand minority members are stopped and searched as compared to sixteen white for every one thousand whites. Although ethnic minorities reflect only 6 percent of the population, they are 10 percent of all stop and searches.

Some have argued that blacks are more often stopped and searched because they are in fact more likely to commit street crime. However, only 11 percent of the stop and searches against ethnic minorities prove positive compared to a similarly low figure of 8 percent for whites.[161] This three percent difference in successful searches between whites and blacks does not justify the intensity with which police search blacks. Stopping more blacks does not lead to *proportionally* more arrests of criminals. It is not a policy that can legitimately claim sufficient positive effects.

A Scotland Yard inquiry found that black people are stopped by the police five times more often than whites. They have a one-in-seven chance of being picked up compared to one-in-thirty-two chance for whites. Of the inquiry's sample of 250,000 individuals stopped, only one-in-nine were successfully arrested, indicating again that random stops are not successful.

Human Rights Watch/Helsinki recognizes and appreciates the words of Commander Mike Briggs who led the investigation:

> There is no doubt that black people are disproportionately stopped. A hit rate of one arrest for every nine stops is not good enough... It can be counter-productive, especially if you get people being stopped on a number of occasions. It can alienate them, making it less likely that they will help us in the future when we may be looking for witnesses, for example. We are now examining ways of putting these matters right.[162]

---

[161] Figures based on November-December 1993; Terry Kirby, "Howard favours wider stop-and-search powers," *The Independent*, March 21, 1994; *Manchester Evening News*, November 15, 1994.

[162] *Sunday Express*, January 21, 1996.

Stop and searches are often abusive and are experienced by young black youth as one more example of widespread racial harassment and prejudice. The ongoing prejudice and mistreatment are especially disturbing because they further exacerbate already tense relations between the police and minority communities. Abusive treatment by police sparked riots in urban areas during the 1980s.

Farouk, a fifteen-year-old, reported:

> If I am with a bunch of white guys I have never been stopped I can tell you that, never, but if I am with a bunch of Asian youths we have been stopped and searched and asked questions. Sometimes you get once or twice or three or four times a day and they don't find anything on you. They say, "You are lucky this time son, but next time we'll get you." They assume that every Asian kid in this area has got to be guilty of something.[163]

Similarly, **Abjol** reported to Human Rights Watch/Helsinki that:

> We get stopped almost every day, just for walking the streets. You get so angry. I am not a criminal, but they treat you like one. All of me mates hate the police because we get harassed by them all the time.[164]

In a case typical of the numerous reports received by Human Rights Watch/Helsinki of a general police presumption of the guilt of non-whites, in February 1995, **Michael Leary**, a senior university lecturer, was waiting for his friend at 8 p.m. At 8:30 two white men approached him, produced badges identifying them as plainclothes police officers. They said they had seen him hanging around and were going to take him to Brixton police station and search him for drugs. His friend arrived and told the officers that she was scheduled to meet Mr. Leary.

> They started pushing and pulling me around. When I refused to take my hands out of my pockets the youngest officer got the

---

[163] From Conference on Young Bengalis and the Criminal Justice System in Tower Hamlets, February 10, 1993.

[164] Human Rights Watch/Helsinki interview, London, July 13, 1995.

handcuffs and forced them on me. One of the officers called for back-up after which three police cars and a police van arrived. I was pushed and manhandled into a car with four officers. I said there was no need to use force and one of the officers told me to "shut up" as I was a piece of dirt and they caught me red-handed.

Once at the station he was forced to strip and was searched for drugs. They found nothing.[165]

Police Behavior/Racism

Non-whites in the U.K. repeatedly expressed the view to Human Rights Watch/Helsinki that the police are racists, and that much of the abuse reported in the sections above is due to police officers' view that non-whites are subhuman or are mere criminals. In 1994, whites filed 76 percent of all the complaints against the police, while 18 percent were filed by blacks or Asians.[166] Since ethnic minorities represent only about 5 percent of the total population, these groups are over represented by about 300 percent. Complaints filed to the London Metropolitan Police show a similar pattern with 30 percent of all complaints being made in 1992 by Afro-Caribbeans or Asians, yet these groups only represent 15 percent of the Greater London population. Another set of statistics shows that "black people are four times more likely to make a complaint, but less likely than whites to have them upheld."[167]

In addition to this bias, the PCA heard numerous cases specifically related to racial discrimination. There were 362 complaints of racially discriminatory behavior in the period from April 1, 1994, to March 31, 1995. This is a 25 percent increase from the 291 complaints made in 1993.[168]

---

[165]Jason Bennetto, "Arrest of black lecturer heightens distrust," *The Independent*, April 17, 1995.

[166] 13 percent Afro-Caribbean, 3 percent Asian, 2 percent "other." Annual Report of the Police Complaints Authority 1994/95 (London: HMSO, Police Complaints Authority, 1995) p. 19.

[167]David Rose and Ken Hyder, "Sacked PC Given New Job by Met," *The Observer*, November 27, 1994.

[168] The findings of these complaints are discussed later.

It is rare for incidents of clear racist sentiments by the police to become public, even though many Afro-Caribbeans and Asians report experiencing such views on a regular basis. It is often difficult to prove racism because there are rarely witnesses available to corroborate the victim's testimony or other means to show the police officer's intent. For this reason, when clear incidents of police racism do become public they are particularly important, because they are brief windows into police behavior that normally takes place in dark streets or areas of detention. The following case is particularly disturbing:

In April 1995, a group of police officers arranged a comedy night fund raiser with Bernard Manning who is well-known for his racially inflammatory jokes. The following is an excerpt from the event that was taped by a television crew for World In Action:

> They knock the fuck out of them coons, eh? Them Los Angeles police units with that fucking nigger on the floor. Fuck me that's not on. Not enough police there." [laughter, banging on the tables, rolling in the aisles]

> They [Asians] believe this because they are born here. They actually think they are English, because they are fucking born here. That means if a dog's born in a stable it's a fucking horse. [Laughter]

> A Liverpool docker went over to South Africa for a job. He says these credentials we couldn't fault [because] its people like you we want over here. We have a lot of trouble with the blacks. He says "we've got a few in Liv' but its not the same we don't fucking bother with them. He says what do we do then? I'll give you a bit of a test then. Go and shoot six niggers and a rabbit. He says what have I got to shoot the rabbit for? He says you've got the fucking job." [laughter][169]

Addressing a black officer present Mr. Manning said, "Isn't this better than swinging through the trees? Having a night out with nice people. You're

---

[169] Text submitted to Human Rights Watch/Helsinki by World in Action.

black, I'm white. Do you think it makes any difference what colour you are? You bet your bollocks it does."[170]

In his defense, the police officer who organized the event said, "Well, you know, homosexuals, coloreds, Irish, foreigners, child abusers, pedophiles, and wife-beaters. Bernard will attack ALL these minorities." [171]

Sponsoring Mr. Manning at a police event can hardly be seen as an honest effort by the police to correct the widespread impression among ethnic minorities that they are bigoted and abusive.

Minority police officers are frequently the brunt of such racist views. They may suffer daily harassment as well as discrimination in job promotion.

PC Joginder Singh Prem, thirty-nine years old, won £25,000 in compensation for being the target of racial slurs made by fellow officers, and for being passed over for promotion during his ten years on the force in Nottinghamshire. PC Prem charged that he was racially discriminated against by being blocked five times for a promotion even though he passed the exams for inspector, harassed by close inspections to which white officers were not subjected, and that he was unfairly criticized and denigrated or ignored in front of colleagues.[172]

According to statements by PC Prem, a police chief called him a "Paki bastard, turnip head and table cloth head." In other instances he was told that he was "just a Paki and only good for cheap work." PC Prem stated:

> These kinds of comments came from high-ranking officers. It was the senior officers who did much to destroy my career. The final straw was when I saw white officers with less service and experience than myself being promoted over my head. I was called all sorts of derogatory remarks, many of a racist nature.

---

[170] Heather Mills, "Action ruled out over Manning's racist cabaret," *The Independent*, April 25, 1995; David Lister and Heather Mills, "Police were secretly taped cheering as a black officer was baited," *The Independent*, April 25, 1995.

[171] Eddie Holt, "The laughing racist policeman," *The Irish Times*, April 29, 1995.

[172] Police Review, May 7, 1993.

The ordinary rank and file were behind me and were sympathetic to my case... but senior officers tried to destroy my career and my records were doctored.[173]

In a letter to the tribunal, Nottinghamshire Chief Constable Dan Crompton admitted officers discriminated against PC Prem's promotion requests, and "there was an unfair accumulation of unfair documents in PC Prem's personnel file and that an unfair impression of PC Prem had been placed in the minds of some other officers."[174]

Sgt. Anil Patani, thirty-four years old, and Sgt. Satinda Sharma, thirty-two years old, were also awarded 5,000 pounds each by a tribunal which found that they had been discriminated against and that racist language had permeated, to some extent, most levels of the force."[175]

Despite this finding and Chief Constable Crompton's admission, an inquiry later cleared the officers in question of racially discriminatory behavior.[176]

PC Michael Reid, a white police officer working in Greater Manchester, made a fourteen-page complaint against three fellow officers. The report charged that the officers, who were part of an initiative to improve race relations, trivialized racist attacks and complaints of racism against the police. The report said that these officers held "negative" attitudes toward ethnic minorities.

---

[173] "Pounds 25.000 for race taunt Asian PC," *The Daily Telegraph,* May 5, 1993; James Golden, "Sikh Who Promoted the Force Wins Pounds 25,000 Damages," *Daily Mail,* May 5, 1993; "Race bias PC wins 25,000 pounds," *The Independent,* May 5, 1993.

[174] Ibid.

[175] David Graves, "18 Police Cleared After Two-Year Racism," *The Daily Telegraph,* August 23, 1994.

[176]Aubrey Chalmers, "Outrage over 1 million pounds racism fiasco," *Daily Mail,* August 23, 1994; "Policemen cleared of racism," *Daily Mail,* August 23, 1994; Graves David, "18 Police Cleared After Two-Year Racism Inquiry," *The Daily Telegraph,* August 23, 1994; Jason Bennetto, "Officers Cleared of Racism After 1 Million Pound Inquiry," *The Independent,* August 23, 1994; "Police Inquiry Clears 18 Officers of Racism Towards Colleague," *The Guardian,* August 23, 1994.

Following an investigation by the PCA into PC Reid's allegations, two officers were charged with discreditable conduct, one officer will be charged with neglect of duty, and a senior officer will face informal disciplinary action.[177]

Failure to Punish Police Misconduct

There are very few cases in which police officers are disciplined for racially discriminatory behavior or racial violence. There is no legal recourse for victims of racial violence and harassment whose cases were not effectively investigated to file complaints against the police for failing in their duty or for racial bias that would result in disciplinary action.

The Police Complaints Authority directs investigations and hears cases against the police. However, the PCA has failed to deal satisfactorily with many of the complaints of racially motivated police conduct. There are far more complaints of police misconduct and particularly racially discriminatory behavior than there are disciplinary actions taken against officers. The PCA and numerous solicitors agree that this difference is an indication that the system of processing complaints is not effective. The lack of disciplinary actions cannot be wholly accounted for by unproven false claims.

COMPLAINTS OF RACIALLY
DISCRIMINATORY BEHAVIOR MADE TO THE PCA

	Complaints	Insufficient/ conflicting evidence	Disciplinary Charges	Dispensed with
1995/96[178]	397	186	4	203
1994/95	362	194	1	162
1993	291	164	1	118
1992[179]	67			
1991[180]	49			

---

[177] "Ethnic monitor police are accused of harassment," *The Daily Telegraph*, November 22, 1994; Ray King, "UK:Race Row Police Will Be Charged - Four Face Internal Action," *Manchester Evening News*, November 21, 1994.

[178] Police Complaints Authority, *Annual Report 1995 - 1996* (London:HMSO, 1996), Table 4.

[179] "Police Report Fewer Overall Complaints in 1993 but Rises in Race and Injury Complaints Grow," *Hermes - UK Government Press Releases*, March 28, 1994.

[180] Duncan Campbell, "Sharp Rise in Claims of Race Bias by Police," *The Guardian*, March 29, 1994.

In its own annual report the PCA stated, "In 1992 no charges were brought against any of the officers involved in investigations. In 1993 disciplinary action was taken in approximately 4 percent of investigated complaints alleging racial discrimination. This was well below the overall level of 10 percent in all investigated complaints considered by the Authority."[181]

There were two reasons offered for this breakdown in the complaints system: 1) improper investigations by the police into their own misconduct, and 2) standards of evidence that were so high that difficult-to-prove cases went unpunished.

There is reason for significant concern that the PCA is not sufficiently independent from the police themselves so as to ensure that cases of police misconduct are effectively investigated. Although the PCA is a full-time body, whose members come from various backgrounds outside the police force, its duties are limited to directing investigations. The actual investigations are carried out by officers who may be, have been or will be affiliated with the police and may even have close ties to those officials under scrutiny. Complaints against the police are, therefore, not investigated independently. While the PCA considers the independent directors' body sufficient, Human Rights Watch/Helsinki believes that confidence cannot be restored in the objectivity of the investigative process as long as police remain at the center of the investigation. [182]

The Human Rights Committee for the International Covenant on Civil and Politics Rights stated in its report:

> The Committee is concerned that, notwithstanding establishment
> in the United Kingdom of mechanisms for external supervision
> of investigations of incidents in which the police or military are
> allegedly involved, especially incidents that result in death or
> wounding persons, the investigations are still carried out by the
> police, and therefore they lack sufficient credibility.[183]

Finally, it is commonly reported that police officers who mean well have great difficulty in reporting or testifying against fellow officers due to the

---

[181] Police Complaints Authority, *Annual Report 1993* (London: HMSO, 1993) p. 41.

[182]Andrew Woodcock, "UN Race Group Raps 'Police Brutality'," *Press Association Newsfile*, March 15, 1996.

[183] p. 3.13

professional culture of policing which values loyalty to other officers above legality and commitments to the broader society. As the previous chart indicates, the PCA's response creates the impression that complaints will not be properly handled and that police misconduct will not be punished appropriately.

The PCA, solicitors and many others have frequently stated that the standards of evidence to carry out disciplinary action against offending officers is too high. Under the current system, it must be proved "beyond a reasonable" doubt that the accused officers took part in misconduct in order to be disciplined.

Because the corroborating witnesses are rarely available, and the police involved can effectively hide or manipulate evidence, this standard of proof is exceedingly high and almost impossible to satisfy. Moreover, this same standard is applied to all accusations regardless of their severity.

As a result, attempts to create a system to insure police accountability have been seriously hampered.

In a survey conducted by the PCA the following public opinions of the PCA were found: 39 percent regarded the PCA as independent, 37 regarded the PCA as impartial, 32 percent thought that the PCA always favored the police, 37 percent trusted the police to carry out inquires into police misconduct fairly.[184]

Police Membership

While the diversity of the police force has improved over the years, it is still not representative of the total population. This has remained a significant concern at least since 1986. In 1989, the Home Office warned that recruitment efforts were lagging and recommended a "genuine commitment to increase the proportion of police officers from ethnic minorities to match the proportion of the local population."[185] Despite this, improvements have not been sufficient. A more ethnically representative police force is necessary to gain trust in the eyes of ethnic minorities.

---

[184] Police Complaints Authority, *Annual Report 1995-96* (London: HMSO, 1996), p.68.

[185] Racial Attacks and Harassment [First report: Session 1989-90], (London:HMSO), section HC 17, para. 20.

ETHNIC MINORITIES IN POLICE FORCE[186]

	England and Wales			Metropolitan Police (London)	
Year	No. Ethnic Minority Recruits	Percent and # officers from Ethnic Minorities		No. Ethnic Minority Recruits	Percent and # officers from Ethnic Minorities
1986	175	0.74%	898	64	1.23%
1987	282	0.89%	1,105	114	1.52%
1988	185	0.96%	1,209	66	1.52%
1989	202	1.03%	1,308	35	1.56%
1990	188	1.08%	1,374	71	1.70%
1991	221	1.23%	1,568	81	1.93%
1992	227	1.35%	1,730	57	2.10%
1993	NA	1.53%	1,908	73	2.41%

In 1995, of a total 127,222 officers, 2,223 were black representing only 1.75 percent. Of those black officers, 158 were sergeants, thirty-six were inspectors, eight chief inspectors, and one was a superintendent. In the Metropolitan Police area, 797 officers were ethnic minorities, or 2.9 percent of the 27,395 total.[187]

ETHNIC MINORITY OFFICERS AND THEIR RANK[188]

Rank	1990	1991	1992
ACPO ranks	0	0	0
Chief Superintendent	0	1	1
Superintendent	4	5	3
Chief Inspector	3	2	4
Inspector	16	22	23
Sergeant	82	92	111
Constable	1320	1445	1602

---

[186] Home Affairs Committee, 3rd Report: Racial Attacks and Harassment, Vol. 1, 1994.

[187] "Race, Discrimination and The Criminal Justice System," submitted to Human Rights Watch/Helsinki from the Association of Black Probation Officers, August 1996.

[188] Ibid.

Positive Steps

As mentioned earlier, in 1993, Chief Police Constable Paul Condon stated in his first major speech to a conference on racial and sexual harassment that "the police must be intolerant of those who indulge in racial abuse, and intolerant of those who use hatred and violence as the tools of their own expression. But if we are to be intolerant of those outside the police service who fail to treat their fellow human beings with dignity and respect, we must be equally intolerant of our own colleagues who fail to reach the required standards."[189]

On July 11, 1996, Home Secretary Michael Howard announced that he would introduce new measures to improve police disciplinary hearings in 1997.[190] Most importantly, the reforms follow the advice of the Police Complaints Authority to develop a less strenuous standard of proof than "beyond a reasonable doubt" for police disciplinary cases. The new standard would allow for a sliding scale standard of proof with strict standards for serious violations, and less severe standards for minor infringements. This could be an important step in the right direction. If this measure is implemented, it may help to make the police more accountable for their behavior and begin to rebuild the trust lost by those who feel victimized by them.[191]

Racial Incidents Units (RIU) have been established in some police departments to focus special attention on racist violence. In some cases these initiatives appear to have positive effects. For example, in Plumstead, where an RIU was established and has been frequently viewed as a success story, the clear-up rate is about 43 percent compared to London's average of 22 percent for cases of racially motivated violence. As of 1995, however, only twelve of sixty-three Metropolitan Police Divisions had RIUs.

In addition to the small percentage of police divisions that have RIUs, a number of concerns have been raised. Some police officers believe that racist attacks and harassment should be handled exclusively by RIUs and thus shirk their own responsibilities. According to Dev Berreh of the Greenwich Action

---

[189] Police Review, March 5, 1993.

[190] At the time of this writing, these measures have been proposed, but not yet made law.

[191] Duncan Campbell, "Sharp Rise in Claims of Race Bias by Police," *The Guardian,* March 29, 1994; John Deane, "Shake-up for Police Discipline System," *Press Association Newsfile,* July 11, 1996.

Committee Against Racist Attacks (GACARA), "They just take any opportunity to pass it on to someone else. They just do not want to deal with racial cases."[192]

RIUs often consist of only a small number of officers who must handle many complaints ranging from low level harassment to violent attacks every day. Human Rights Watch/Helsinki attempted to contact the highly acclaimed Plumstead station through their hotline five times within a single week, only to reach an answering machine. If officers are pushing racially motivated cases to the RIUs and RIUs are understaffed and therefore, unable to respond, then this otherwise well-intended effort will yield little effective change.

In 1985, the Association of Chief Police Officers (ACPO) issued guiding principles concerning racist attacks. The principles proposed a uniform definition of a racially motivated incident which, if properly implemented nation-wide, could help effective monitoring. In 1986, the Home Office also released its *Good Practice Guidelines for the Police: The Response to Racial Attacks*, which set clear expectations for police behavior and practices critical for handling incidents of racial violence and harassment.

---

[192] Human Rights Watch/Helsinki interview with Dev Berreh of GACARA, London, June 30, 1995; Home Affairs Committee, 3rd Report: Racial Attacks and Harassment, Vol. 1, 1994, p. xiii.

8. THE COURTS

Prosecution of Racist Violence

In January 1992, the CPS amended the Code for Crown Prosecutors to include that "a clear racial motivation will be regarded as an aggravating feature when assessing whether prosecution is required in the public interest."[193] Despite these provisions, numerous solicitors and victim support organizations indicate that in contradiction to their mandate, the CPS does not sufficiently take racial motives into account.

Chris Boothman, legal director for the Commission for Racial Equality, testified for the Home Affairs Committee that "despite [the CPS] making the right kind of noises, we are not convinced that they have the kind of procedures in place to make that commitment a reality."[194]

In addition, a representative from the Greater London Action for Racial Equality testified to the Home Affairs Committee that "it is the experience of our members that the Police have sought to prosecute a number of cases but the CPS has refused to proceed. Prosecutions often do not proceed because the CPS requires an unacceptably high level of certainty that a case is winnable. This leads to a situation where case law is not being established to support such prosecutions."[195]

This issue remains significant despite the fact that the Home Office itself noted several years earlier in 1989/90 that "anecdotal evidence, referred to by the Racial Attacks Group, of occasions where the police strongly recommended prosecutions but were refused by the CPS, or where the CPS lawyers failed to emphasize racial motivation as an aggravating factor to emphasize [when cases] came to court."[196] In light of these findings, the Home Office recommended that the CPS track cases of racist incidents. This was not done until three years later and is not yet thoroughly implemented.

As Lord Chief Justice Taylor of Gosforth stated:

> Race issues go to the heart of our system of justice, which demands that all are treated as equals before the law...It is therefore a matter of the gravest concern if members of the

---

[193] Home Affairs Committee, *3rd Report*, p. xxii.

[194] Ibid., p. 47. Q.316.

[195] Ibid., p. 201.

[196] Ibid., p.73. Q.480.

ethnic minorities feel they are discriminated against by the criminal justice system: more so if their fears were to be borne out in reality...Members of the ethnic minorities (whose confidence in the system may be at best tenuous) are likely to perceive the entire edifice [of the criminal justice system] as one integrated whole: one system of criminal justice which, too often, simply appears to be stacked against them. Because of this, it is not acceptable for the various agencies to try to shuffle the blame for any discrimination onto each other....A Bangladeshi youth is attacked by skinheads: his parents think it not worth bothering to report the incident to the police, since they believe nothing will be done. The black victim of a burglary attends court to give evidence in the trial and the staff assume he is the defendant and treat him as such...These commonplace examples (and they can be multiples) show the ways in which our system is manifestly failing those it is supposed to protect either through tolerating attitudes and assumptions which are fundamentally racist, or through allowing a section of the population to believe it is beyond the protection of the criminal law.[197]

Racial Bias in Sentencing

Determining whether the entire British criminal justice system suffers from biased sentencing is very difficult with the information currently available. Although ethnic minorities make up about 5 percent of the total population, these groups are 16.2 percent of the prison population. The reasons behind this almost 300 percent over-representation are notoriously difficult to untangle and beyond the scope of this report.

Despite these difficulties there is evidence that some individual courts have been consistently biased in their sentencing. There is further anecdotal evidence and limited statistical evidence to suggest that there is a significant racial bias in the criminal justice process that systematically prosecutes more ethnic minorities, with higher sentences than whites for similar crimes, and with less opportunities for bail.

A study that compared sentencing practices between blacks and whites found that in some courts blacks received harsher sentencing for similar crimes.

---

[197] "UK: Lord Chancellor's Department - Lord Chief Justice Speaks on Race and Criminal Justice," *Hermes - UK Government Press Releases*, October 14, 1994.

In Dudley, for example, blacks had a 23 percent greater chance of receiving a prison sentence than whites in similar circumstances. Thus, instead of an expected 131 out of 246 black offenders to go to prison, 161 received prison sentences. In cases where there were black co-defendants, 71 percent were imprisoned compared with only 25 percent for whites. The study concluded that 20 percent of the over-representation of blacks in prison could be attributed to biased treatment.[198]

Equal justice is central to a fair and sustainable democracy. Without clear evidence that there is in fact equal justice, already deep frustrations among ethnic minorities about police behavior and suspicions about unequal treatment before the law will fester and continue to fuel mistrust.

The words of Lord Chief Justice Taylor of Gosforth are appreciated as a call for more careful monitoring: "What we principally suffer, is a lack of hard information which would allow us to know where, and to what extent, racial discrimination is present...all agencies should move quickly to a common, and comprehensive, system of data collection...in my view it is profoundly important if we are to uphold public confidence in the administration of justice."[199]

Court Membership

As with the police, the near total absence of minorities in judicial posts is viewed as further evidence that state institutions are unreceptive to non-whites. In March 1996, the National Association of Probation Officers and the Association of Black Probation Officers conducted a study of the diversity of the criminal justice system. Below are some of their findings[200]:

---

[198] Roger Hood, *A Question of Judgement, Summary of Race and Sentencing: A Study in the Crown Court* (London: Commission for Racial Equality, 1992).

[199] "UK: Lord Chancellor's Department - Lord Chief Justice Speaks on Race and Criminal Justice," *Hermes - UK Government Press Releases*, June 30, 1995.

[200] Document titled, "Race, Discrimination and The Criminal Justice System," submitted to Human Rights Watch/Helsinki from the Association of Black Probation Officers, August 1996.

JUDICIAL POSTS[201]

	1992		1995	
	Total	Ethnic Origin	Total	Ethnic Origin
High Court Judges	82	0	95	0
Circuit Judges	480	3	514	5
District Judges	257	0	339	2
Recorders	784	7	897	13
Assistant	475	8	341	9
Total	2,078	18	2,086	29

CROWN PROSECUTION SERVICE

Grade 1995	Total	Ethnic Minority	Percent
Grade 1-6	248	4	1.6
Legal Assistants	1255	90	7.1
Executive Officers	1327	77	5.8

Liberty reported that in 1991 an estimated 6 percent of all solicitors were members of ethnic minority groups and there were no ethnic minorities represented among the Law Lords, Court of Appeal judges, or High Court judges.

In 1992 it was discovered that ethnic minorities failed their Bar exams at a rate of 44.7 percent compared to 16 percent for whites. The discrepancy led to an investigation by Dame Jocelyn Barrow. She concluded that there was "no direct or indirect racial discrimination as defined by the Race Relations Act" against ethnic minority students. However, there was a "significant link" between those who found traineeships and success in the Bar exams, and that ethnic minorities were "substantially less likely" to be offered training positions in chambers.

Only 48 percent of ethnic minority students were given traineeships, compared to 70 percent for whites. According to the report, these differences could not be accounted for by differences in academic achievement alone.

In 1994, the success rate for ethnic minorities rose to 70 percent, while the success rate for whites was 88 percent. A further analysis of the lesser, but

---

[201] Data on the ethnic background of members of the judiciary was not available until 1992.

continuing disparity was requested by Mr. Graham Hamer, registrar of the Council of Legal Education, who administers the exams.[202]

Positive Steps

A number of positive steps have been taken over recent years to improve the way courts deal with cases of racial discrimination and racist violence. For example, the inquiry into possible racial discrimination by barristers' chambers concluded with these positive recommendations: "More clear criteria for passing or failing and the right to take the bar exams again within six months; external examiners and double marking; teacher training for staff and more regular informal assessment of students work; a students' union; a remedial skills tutor; an equal opportunities officer."[203]

Racial Equality Councils are funded by the Commission for Racial Equality and local authorities to provide information and advice to victims of racist violence and harassment. As of 1994, there were eighty-seven throughout Britain.[204] These institutions have the potential to impact positively on race relations and respond to racist violence. The effectiveness of these organizations, however, varies widely according to the strength and commitments of the staff in each council.

The case of **Kenneth Harris**, thirty-two, was an excellent example of how taking racial motivation into account can generate more appropriate sentencing. He was attacked by three white men with screwdrivers. He was stabbed, kicked and his legs were twice run over by a car. Vincent Brian Ribbans, 25, Edward Michael Duggan, 26, Laurie Christopher Ridley, 22, admitted causing grievous bodily harm

---

[202] Robert Rice, "Discrimination seen in Bar training," *Financial Times*, April 13, 1994; Robert Rice, "Race link reported in Bar training," *Financial Times*, April 13, 1994; Clare Dyer, "Bar's Law School May Face Court," *The Guardian*, April 23, 1994; Jason Bennetto, "Black law students suffering jobs bias," *The Independent*, April 21, 1994; "Leading Article: Equal opportunities in barrister training," *The Independent*, April 13, 1994; Clare Dyer, "All that We've Ever Asked for is a Level Playing Field," *The Guardian*, April 13, 1994; Frances Gibb, "Race bias 'hampers black Bar students'," *The Times*, April 13, 1994; Gavin Cordon, "Reports Warns Over Race Discrimination in Chambers," *Press Association Newsfile*, April 12, 1994. The Society of Black Lawyers questioned the inquiry's independence and criticized it for focusing on lower levels of academic achievement among ethnic minorities. That debate is not within the scope of this report.

[203] Ibid.

[204] Home Affairs Committee, 3rd Report: Racial Attacks and Harassment, Vol. 1, 1994, p. xxii.

with intent, but denied attempted murder. They approached Mr. Harris and his girlfriend, Lynn Woodward, pelting them with chips and verbally abusing her for having a black boyfriend, saying that she was a "nigger lover and wog meat." When Mr. Ridley began kicking their car, Mr Harris asked what the problem was. Mr. Ridley said the problem was that Mr. Harris was black. Mr. Ribbans grabbed Mr. Harris from behind while the others kicked, punched and stamped on him. Mr. Ridley jumped into Mr. Harris' car. His friends chanted, "Run him over, run him over." Mr. Ridley reversed the car driving over Mr. Harris.

During the investigation, a German Iron Cross, a jeweled Nazi Swastika, and racist literature were found at Mr. Ridley's home. Judge Smedly QC, at the Central Criminal Court, sentenced Mr. Duggan to three years of imprisonment, Mr. Ridley to five years, and Mr. Ribbans to three years. The Attorney-General considered the sentences unduly lenient due to the horrific nature of the attack. The new sentences given were seven years for Mr. Ridley, and five years for Mr. Ribbans and Mr. Duggan. [205]

Training has been provided for judges under Justice Potter. A new two-year program will require 1,750 circuit judges, recorders and assistant recorders to attend seminars or training days, involving an overnight stay, to combat racial stereotyping and prejudice.

---

[205]"Law Report: Racial Motive to Crime Justifies a Stiffer Sentence," *The Guardian*, November 28, 1994; Peter Rose, "Black Man Crippled Because he had a White Girlfriend," *Daily Mail*, June 21, 1994; "Engineer run over in race attack," *The Independent*, June 21, 1994; "Racist Three Jailed after Man Run Over," *The Guardian*, June 21, 1994; Paul Cheston, "Gang Jailed for 'Appalling; Race Attack," *Evening Standard*, June 20, 1994; "Gang run man over in racial attack at garage," *The Independent*, October 19, 1993; "Race gang beat and ran over driver," *The Times*, October '9, 1993.

9. THE LEGAL CONTEXT

International Law

Rights to non-discrimination in the application of international standards

The United Kingdom is a party to the International Covenant on Civil and Political Rights (ICCPR)[206], which requires that:

> Each State Party to the present Covenant undertakes to respect and to ensure to all individuals within its territory and subject to its jurisdiction the rights recognized in the present Covenant without distinction of any kind, such as race, color, sex, language, religion, political or other opinion, national or social origin, property, birth or other status.[207]

The ICCPR also requires government authorities to treat minorities equally and to take positive measures to prevent discrimination.

> All persons are equal before the law and are entitled without any discrimination to the equal protection of the law. In this respect, the law shall prohibit any discrimination and guarantee to all persons equal and effective protection against discrimination on any ground such as race, color, sex, language, religion, political or other opinion, national or social origin, property, birth or other status.[208]

Among the other rights that must be ensured without discrimination under the ICCPR are: freedom from torture or cruel, inhuman or degrading treatment or punishment (Article 7), freedom from the arbitrary deprivation of life (Article 6), freedom from arbitrary arrest or detention (Article 9), freedom to choose a residence within a country (Article 12), freedom from arbitrary or unlawful interference with privacy, family, and home, and the right to the protection of the

---

[206] Signed by the United Kingdom on September 16, 1968, and ratified on May 20, 1976.

[207] United Nations International Covenant on Civil and Political Rights, Article 2(1).

[208] Ibid., Article 26.

law against such interference (Article 16). Yet, as this report documents, these rights and others are routinely denied to minorities in the United Kingdom.

Although the UK is a party to the ICCPR, it has declined to sign the Optional Protocol. As a result, human rights violations cannot be brought by individuals to the United Nations Human Rights Committee for consideration. However, though the United Kingdom has not permitted the international community to use this enforcement mechanism, the country is nonetheless bound to its promise to uphold these rights of its citizens.

Similarly, the U.K. has ratified the European Convention for the Protection of Human Rights and Fundamental Freedoms (ECHR), which states that:

> The enjoyment of the rights and freedoms set forth in this Convention shall be secured without discrimination on any ground such as sex, race, color, language, religion, political or other opinion, national or social origin, association with a national minority, property, birth or other status.[209]

Again, although the UK is internationally bound by the European Convention for the Protection of Human Rights and Fundamental Freedoms (ECHR), the Convention has not been incorporated into domestic law.

The United Kingdom has also ratified the United Nations International Convention on the Elimination of All Forms of Racial Discrimination (CERD), in which state parties commit themselves:

> To prohibit and to eliminate racial discrimination in all its forms and to guarantee the right of everyone, without distinction as to race, color, or national origin, to equality before the law, notably in the enjoyment of . . . the right to equal treatment before the tribunals . . . the right to security of person and protection by the State against violence or bodily harm, whether inflicted by government officials or by any individual, group, or institution . . .[210]

---

[209] The European Convention on Human Rights, Article 14.

[210] United Nations International Convention on the Elimination of All Forms of Racial Discrimination (CERD), Article 5(b). Signed by the United Kingdom on October 11, 1966, and ratified on March 7, 1969.

The Convention on the Elimination of All Forms of Racial Discrimination also sets out parties' obligation to provide an effective remedy to those individuals whose fundamental rights have been violated:

> States Parties shall assure to everyone within their jurisdiction effective protection and remedies, through the competent national tribunals and other State institutions, against any acts of racial discrimination which violates his human rights and fundamental freedoms contrary to this Convention, as well as the right to seek from such tribunals just and adequate reparation or satisfaction for any damage suffered as a result of such discrimination.[211]

Responsibility of the state to respond to racial violence

There are features of international law that are particularly relevant to the problem of racial violence and the responsibilities of the state to respond. The International Covenant on Civil and Political Rights, as noted above, ensures that all people are treated equally by the law. Thus, ethnic minorities that are victims of racial violence are entitled to equal protection and treatment by law enforcement officials. Articles (1) and 26 (quoted above) have been violated in many of the cases highlighted above.

Law enforcement obligations under international law further reinforce this responsibility:

- Law enforcement officials shall at all times fulfill the duty imposed upon them by law, by serving the community and by protecting all persons against illegal acts, consistent with the high degree of responsibility required by their profession. [Article 1, United Nations Code of Conduct for Law Enforcement Officials, G.A. Res. 169, U.N. GAOR, 34th Sess., Supp. No. 46 at 186, U.N. Doc. A/34/46 (1980).]

- In performance of their duty, law enforcement officials shall respect and protect human dignity and maintain and uphold the human rights of all persons. [Article 2, United Nations Code of Conduct for Law Enforcement Officials]

---

[211] CERD, Article 6.

International codes of practice also require that violations of these laws are properly reviewed and punished:

- Every law enforcement agency...should be held to the duty of disciplining itself... and the actions of law enforcement officials should be responsive to public scrutiny. [Preamble, United Nations Code of Conduct for Law Enforcement Officials.]

Article 12 of the U.N. Convention against Torture and other Cruel, Inhuman or Degrading Treatment or Punishment requires "prompt and impartial investigation" of charges of mistreatment.

Article 2 of the ECHR states that the "deprivation of life shall not be regarded as inflicted in contravention of this article when it results of the use of force which is no more than absolutely necessary: a) in defense of any person from unlawful violence; b) in order to effect a lawful arrest or to prevent the escape of a person lawfully detained..."

Article 9(4) of the ICCPR states "Anyone who is deprived of his liberty by arrest or detention shall be entitled to take proceedings before a court, in order that the court may decide without delay on the lawfulness of his detention and order his release if the detention is not lawful."

Article 5(4) of the ECHR and Principle 32 of the United Nations Body of Principles for the Protection of All Persons Under Any Form of Detention or Imprisonment contain similar guarantees.

National Law

The UK does not have a written constitution or bill of rights. Although individuals are protected by legislation and codes of practice, freedoms recognized as "human rights" under international standards are not rights given any special level of protection.

British law provides a number of legal tools specifically relevant to cases of racial violence in addition to standard laws covering crimes such as criminal damage, arson, riot, violent disorder, affray, various assault charges, manslaughter, and murder. These specific laws include :

- the Prevention of Terrorism Act, which precludes: "The use of violence for political ends and includes any use of violence for the purpose of putting the public or any section of the public in fear."

- the Local Government Act 1972, section 222, which gives local authorities the power to "prosecute or defend or appear in any legal proceedings" if they believe that this will promote or protect "the interests of the inhabitants of their area." Authorities can take legal action in cases of racial harassment. The section allows authorities to bring criminal proceedings against perpetrators of racial harassment, obtain injunctions to prevent public nuisance, obtain injunctions to prevent obstruction of authority's statutory duties, appear in legal proceedings brought by others, and/or obtain injunctions to prevent criminal offenses.

- the Protection from Eviction Act 1977, section 1(3), declares as an offense doing anything likely to interfere with the peace or comfort of a "residential occupier" or his or her family if: the acts were done to make them give up the premises or to refrain from doing something they are entitled to do which is related to the premises.

There are also a number of laws that deal specifically with racial harassment:

- "Fear or Provocation of Violence," section 4(1), makes it an offense to use threatening, abusive or insulting words or behavior to someone else in the following cases: make them believe that violence will be used against them immediately; provoke the immediate use of violence; when that person is likely to believe that violence will be provoked; when it actually is likely that violence will be provoked.

It is also an offense to distribute or display a threatening, abusive, or insulting "visible representation" to someone else in the circumstances listed above. The maximum penalty under these sections is six months of imprisonment or a fine not exceeding £5,000, or both.

- Under "Harassment, Alarm or Distress," section 5(1), it is an offense: "[to] use threatening, abusive, or insulting words or behavior, or disorderly behavior, within the hearing or sight of a person likely to be caused harassment, alarm, or distress as a result. or to display a visual representation with the same effect." The maximum punishment under this section is a fine not exceeding £1,000.

•   Harassment with Intent was introduced in the Criminal Justice and Public Order Act 1994 and is similar to section 5(1) above, but the prosecution must show intent to harass, alarm or distress. Although more difficult to prosecute, the maximum penalty for this offenses is six months of imprisonment and/or a £5,000 fine.

There are also laws against inciting racial hatred. The consent of the attorney general must be obtained before a prosecution under this legislation can be launched, however, and a number of conditions must also be met in order to prosecute, including that the offense can take place in a private or a public place, but not inside a dwelling where no one outside is affected; and that the accused did intend, and was aware that the material or conduct might be threatening, abusive or insulting. The magistrate can issue a search warrant if there are reasonable grounds to suspect the presence of offensive material. The maximum penalty for offenses under the incitement of racial hatred laws is two years of imprisonment and/or an unlimited fine.

•   Under Section 18(1) — "Words, Behavior, Display of Written Material" — a person who uses threatening, abusive or insulting words or behavior, or who displays any written material that is threatening, abusive or insulting is guilty of an offense if by doing so he or she intends to stir up racial hatred or is likely to stir up racial hatred.

•   Section 19(1) — "Publishing or Distributing Written Material" — is similar to Section 18(1), but refers to the distribution of such material.

•   Section 23(1) — "Possession of Racially Inflammatory Material" — applies the same criteria to a person who possesses such material and who intends it to be displayed, published, distributed or used for television or radio.

Despite the number of existing codes of practice, a number of solicitors testified that the CPS does not apply them effectively. Additionally, Human Rights Watch/Helsinki shares the concern expressed by Liberty that the practices of immigration control, prison and police services are exempt from the Race Relations Act 1976. This is particularly disturbing in the face of numerous accounts of racially biased police practices such as brutality, harassment, and failing to respond to racial violence.